"This is not just a book *t*
an invitation to *encounter*
monastic tradition that tr
his spirituality, and opene
they are meeting Merton
deepen their understandi
readers will enjoy Bonnie Thurston's conversational style
and benefit from her singular insights into Merton and his
wisdom. This is a book to savor and ponder!"

> —Christine M. Bochen
> Professor Emerita of Religious Studies
> Nazareth College, Rochester, New York
> Co-author of *The Thomas Merton Encyclopedia*

"Thurston argues that to understand Thomas Merton one
must understand him as a monk. This careful study argues
that point with deep insight based on her four decades of
reading and writing about the Merton corpus. This book,
extremely readable and unfailingly intelligent, is highly
recommended."

> —Lawrence S. Cunningham, The University
> of Notre Dame

"One of Bonnie Thurston's great gifts to us is her ability to write, when appropriate, about profound topics with a light touch—both accessible and illuminating. That gift is on full display in this wonderful distillation not only of Thomas Merton's core spiritual teachings but of her many years of study, reflection, and prayer on these teachings. She shows clearly and persuasively how Merton's monastic vocation and vision do not separate him from those outside the cloister, but are the ground for his compassionate, insightful identification with the hopes and needs of people in all walks of life, continuing to resonate and inspire in our day as it did in his."

—Patrick O'Connell
Former president of the International Thomas
Merton Society and editor of *The Merton Seasonal*

Shaped by the End You Live For

Thomas Merton's Monastic Spirituality

Bonnie B. Thurston

Foreword by
Paul Quenon, OCSO

LITURGICAL PRESS
Collegeville, Minnesota

www.litpress.org

Library of Congress Cataloging-in-Publication Data

Names: Thurston, Bonnie Bowman, author.
Title: Shaped by the end you live for : Thomas Merton's monastic
    spirituality / Bonnie Thurston.
Description: Collegeville, Minnesota : Liturgical Press, 2020. | Includes
    bibliographical references. | Summary: "A survey of Thomas
    Merton's thought on fundamental aspects of monastic formation and
    spirituality, which also addresses some of the temptations and popular
    misunderstandings surrounding monastic life"—Provided by publisher.
Identifiers: LCCN 2019040245 (print) | LCCN 2019040246 (ebook) |
    ISBN 9780814688076 (paperback) | ISBN 9780814688328 (epub) |
    ISBN 9780814688328 (mobi) | ISBN 9780814688328 (pdf)
Subjects: LCSH: Merton, Thomas, 1915–1968. | Monastic and religious life.
Classification: LCC BX4705.M542 T58 2020 (print) | LCC BX4705.M542
    (ebook) | DDC 255—dc23
LC record available at https://lccn.loc.gov/2019040245
LC ebook record available at https://lccn.loc.gov/2019040246

In grateful memory:
Sr. Mary David DeFeo, OCSO
and
Br. Patrick Hart, OCSO
They first were holy and we may truly call them so.
The Rule of St. Benedict 4.62.

Contents

Foreword

There are so many aspects to Bonnie Thurston that the author of this study, like Thomas Merton, is hard to fit into one category. Of all the encounters I have had with her over many years, I retain an image of one moment that seems to sum up her profile. It was at one of the Thomas Merton international conferences where I was seated high enough to see the floor of the stage. After her introduction, in strides Bonnie Thurston, fully confident in the midst of academics, experts, scholars from across the country, and every kind of Merton reader. She wore a plain blouse, skirt, gardening shoes, and light gray socks. That said it all. Here was a woman who cultivates a solitary life, tills a garden at her hermitage back in my home state of West Virginia. Of course, she wore no religious habit, but the plain outfit and practical shoes spoke of monastic simplicity. Her tone was as one attending to business, and her content reached to the depths.

This book achieves those qualities both explicitly and implicitly, in the sense that she knows of what she

speaks and speaks by experience. Bonnie is precise, nu-
anced, and profound, yet writes simply and directly. She
meets the highest standards of scholarship and has published widely and often in New Testament studies. In her
scholarly work, her personal life remains out of sight, but
nevertheless it informs her spiritual understanding. As a
thinker she can be one tough-minded West Virginia gal
and I remember her taking down the chair of theology
from a Catholic university after his lecture, offering him
nine points of criticism. His brief and humble response
was he agreed with every point. I am glad it did not
break out into a squabble because the audience was held
in the abbey church here at Gethsemani.

While being a lecturer and author or editor of
twenty-two theological books, she is also a poet. I once
gave her an argument that her poetry reflects too much
of the pedagogue in her. She said that is because she
is a pedagogue. Since then I have seen nothing of the
likes in her poetry. Her poetic sequence on ancient Irish
sites and churches are so sensitive you can feel you are
there, even though you've never been.[1]

She has put it in her own words: "Writing is my authentic prayer, an attempt to articulate the glimpsed

1. Bonnie Bowman Thurston, *Belonging to Borders* (Collegeville,
MN: Liturgical Press, 2011).

"beyond" or "other," to honor God's gratuitous, humanizing gift of language and return the gift to its Giver."[2]

In those poetic works more of the profile and history of her personal life emerges, and how it informs her writing. "I am not a monastic, and have no vocation to cenobitic life, knowing only too well the nightmare I would be to a novice mistress and my sisters. But for nearly thirty years of widowhood, I have experimented with living more or less as a solitary in the old Celtic mode. Without formal vows, I try in a quiet way to conduct my 'ordinary' life monastically."[3]

This small volume is focused on the core of Merton's writing, in terms of themes readers are familiar with—silence, prayer, God's call, renunciation, contemplation. This is a deftly written handbook on the salient points of monastic spirituality fundamental to Merton's writing. By all evidence it is a synopsis of a wide and continuous reading on Merton that began with Bonnie's doctoral dissertation. But in a less obvious way it also springs from a life of solitude lived "in the old Celtic mode."

I am thoroughly familiar with Merton's themes and writings, beginning with my days with him in the novi-

2. Abbey of the Arts, "Featured Poet: Bonnie Thurston," Featured Poet Series, https://abbeyofthearts.com/blog/2019/09/11/featured-poet-bonnie-thurston/.

3. Bonnie Bowman Thurston, *Practicing Silence: New and Selected Verses* (Brewster, MA: Paraclete Press, 2014), xviii.

xii   *Shaped by the End You Live For*

tiate, but nevertheless I find in reading through these pages a lucidity and balance, an engaging counterpoint of themes that does justice to Merton's multifaceted thought yet retains basic simplicity. It is an excellent work for beginners as well as for seasoned readers, helping to refresh the air and regain orientation. Merton had such broad interests and was such a pioneer on many frontiers, you can easily lose the central motifs that were driving his expansive energy. Namely, the search for God in monastic life, the love of the place and the brethren, all of which grew and spread beyond the enclosure walls. It is in the deep roots of this solitude and silence that we find one another, whether friend or stranger, whether Christian or of another faith and practice altogether—or of a faith that cannot name itself.

Merton came to the universal through the particular. It is good to acquaint here, or reacquaint oneself with the particular, to gain the profound but simple grasp on realities that lead unto such agape and inclusive humanity.

Br. Paul Quenon, OCSO

Introduction

Since the 1970s books about Thomas Merton have been a growth industry, never more so than in 2015, the centenary of his birth. As Henri Nouwen noted many years ago in *The Genessee Diary*, "Merton is like the Bible: he can be used for almost any purpose. The conservative and the progressive, the liberal and the radical, those who fight for changes and those who complain about them . . . they all quote Merton to express their ideas and convictions."[1]

This is in part because Merton had so *many* interests and wrote so *much* about most of them. Reflecting in 1964 on "the need for constant self-revision, growth, leaving behind, renunciation of yesterday, yet . . . continuity with all yesterdays," he said of himself, "My ideas are always changing, always moving around one

---

1. Henri J. M. Nouwen, *The Genessee Diary* (New York: Doubleday, 1976), 160.

center, always seeing the center from somewhere else. I will always be accused of inconsistencies."[2]

It is my conviction that, actually, Merton's "one center" was monastic life, that if one does not understand Merton as a monk, one does not understand Merton. This is not the first or only book on Merton-the-monk (see the bibliography that closes this book), but it has been some years since one has addressed the subject. Furthermore, monasticism has a great deal to teach all spiritual pilgrims, perhaps particularly Christian ones, so I have tried throughout this book to highlight how Merton's monastic spirituality "translates" for the rest of us.

I am not a monk, but I have received important spiritual gifts from the Christian monastic tradition, especially from women's monastic communities, with whom I have lived for extended periods as the stranger who was taken in. (You know who you are and have survived.) I have written a bit about monasticism elsewhere[3] and bring my personal experiences of mo-

2. Thomas Merton, *Dancing in the Water of Life: Seeking Peace in the Hermitage*, The Journals of Thomas Merton, vol. 5: *1963–1965*, ed. Robert E. Daggy (San Francisco: HarperSanFrancisco, 1997), 67.

3. Bonnie Bowman Thurston, "Monasticism and Marriage," *Contemplative Review* 17, no. 4 (1984): 6–12; Bonnie Thurston, "*Soli Deo Placere Desiderans,*" in *A Monastic Vision for the 21st Century*, ed. Patrick Hart (Kalamazoo, MI: Cistercian Publications, 2006), 1–22, and *Monastic Life: A Sign of Contradiction to the Fashionable Idols* (Oxford: SLG Press, 2016).

nasticism to over forty years as a student of Merton's thought, about which I have written extensively.

Let me begin in good, German academic fashion by describing what this book is not, beginning with the fact that it is not an academic or strictly scholarly book. Although of necessity there is reference to his life, this is not a biography of Merton. (Suggested biographies appear in the bibliography.) As noted, it is not the first on the subject, nor is it a comprehensive treatment of Merton's monastic spirituality. For example, I don't explicitly discuss Merton's ideas about monastic practices[4] or Merton's deep devotion to Our Lady, to whom all Cistercian houses are dedicated. Merton was one of the founding fathers of monastic interreligious dialogue, which has subsequently developed a spirituality of its own.[5] Herein I do not discuss that important material or Merton's work in ecumenism, his openness to the Orthodox and Protestant traditions of Christianity. There is a growing literature on the spirituality of poetry and on that of work for peace and justice. Again,

4. See Charles Cummings, *Monastic Practices*, rev. ed. (Collegeville, MN: Liturgical Press, 2015). I delight to have had a hand in the revised edition.

5. Interested readers may consult the "Merton and" (Sufism, Buddhism, Judaism, etc.) series published by Fons Vitae Press in Louisville, Kentucky. Fr. Jaechan Anselmo Park, OSB, has recently written a very fine book on Merton and Buddhism, *Thomas Merton's Encounter with Buddhism and Beyond* (Collegeville, MN: Liturgical Press, 2019).

Merton made original contributions to both, which we shall not examine. What I have attempted to do is to highlight what I take to be the crucial or foundational aspects of Merton's peculiarly (in both senses of the word) monastic spirituality.

It might help the reader to know my methods of proceeding. I have tried to let Merton speak for himself, so I use primary source material (what Merton himself wrote) or secondary material from his fellow monastics (both men and women) who know monastic life from the inside. For the extensive secondary material (articles about Merton) the reader may consult the work of Patricia Burton or the Merton Center website, both mentioned in the bibliography. There is a lot of quotation from Merton in this book, all of it written before inclusive language was the norm in discourse. Some readers will find Merton's language in this regard difficult or offensive. I regret that, but I am not free to alter original sources. Nor do I think I know "what Merton would have thought about" subjects he did not explicitly speak to or write about. I do not change the primary sources or speculate about what Merton "might have said."

My rationale and intention in adding another book to the groaning Merton shelf is to make his foundational monastic ideas better known to those outside the monastery, though I hope it might be of some value to monastics, perhaps particularly to novices, precisely because I think those ideas are so valuable and relevant to the world in which we live. (We'll address this explicitly in chapter 4.) To that end I have tried to write informally and conversationally in hopes of "inviting the reader in." Occasionally I have committed a scholarly indiscretion by, for example, filling in a bit of history or delving into the etymology of words. As Merton was in modern languages polylingual, had a command of Latin, and knew some Greek, I hope he wouldn't mind. I do this when the information illuminates what lies behind or beneath Merton's ideas. Forgive me. I hope readers who wish to pursue further one or another of Merton's ideas will find the notes of value. Unless otherwise stated, biblical quotations (of which there are many because the monastic offices are basically biblical) are from the New Revised Standard Version and quotations from The Rule of St. Benedict are from the Fry edition.[6]

I agree with Dom Michael Casey, OCSO, in his essay "Thomas Merton and Monastic Renewal" that "mostly" (as Casey suggests) when Merton "spoke about monasticism he seems to have been thinking about Gethsemani."[7] Merton was formed by his own

---

6. Timothy Fry, ed., *The Rule of St. Benedict* (Collegeville, MN: Liturgical Press, 1981).

7. Michael Casey, "Thomas Merton and Monastic Renewal," *Cistercian Studies Quarterly* 53, no. 2 (2018): 165.

experiences in his own monastery. Thus Merton is not the definitive word on monasticism or monastic spirituality, although, as multiple volumes of his notes and talks in the Monastic Wisdom Series attest, he had done significant research into its origins and development. (See bibliography.) The five areas of reform that Casey suggests were focal for Merton ("more authentic exercise of authority, greater flexibility and adaptability, more seriousness in the practice of monastic discipline, a greater emphasis on solitude, and more openness to interaction with the world"[8]) are areas of perennial concern for monasticism and monastics. You will hear their echo in this book.

Finally, as I was finishing this study, I revisited the summary chapter of Lawrence S. Cunningham's *Thomas Merton and the Monastic Vision* and was delighted to discover that what Cunningham notes as the "three fundamental characteristics . . . of what is implied by the term 'monastic'" that Merton suggested for a talk in India are, in fact, primary themes woven into this book. Briefly they are (1) detachment, (2) "preoccupation . . . with the radical inner depth of one's religious and philosophical beliefs; the grounds of those beliefs; and their spiritual implications," and (3) "concern with inner transformation and . . . consciousness of a tran-

---

8. Casey, "Thomas Merton and Monastic Renewal," 173.

scendent dimension of life beyond the empirical self and of 'ethical and pious observance.'"[9] Each also speaks importantly to the spiritual lives of those of us who are not monastics. I am always delighted when my thinking about Merton concurs with those of other Merton scholars from whom I learn so much. No matter how solitary the writing, no one writes a book alone. This work has been sustained by those who pray for me and by several Merton scholars who over many years have become dear friends and greatly enriched my life, as I hope something in this book might enrich yours.

July 22, 2019
Feast of St. Mary Magdalene
The Anchorage, Wheeling, WV

9. Lawrence S. Cunningham, *Thomas Merton and the Monastic Vision* (Grand Rapids, MI: Eerdmans, 1999), 191 and 192.

Chapter 1

Merton's Call to Monastic Life

Merton opened his long essay "Basic Principles of Monastic Spirituality" with Jesus Christ: "There can be no doubt that the monastic vocation is one of the most beautiful in the Church of God. The 'contemplative life,' as the life of the monastic orders is usually called today, is a life entirely devoted to the mystery of Christ, to living the life of God who gives Himself to us in Christ."[1] He continued, "The great ends of the

---

1. The essay first appeared as a stand-alone pamphlet published by Gethsemani Abbey in 1957, and later as "Basic Principles of Monastic Spirituality" in Thomas Merton, *The Monastic Journey*, ed. Patrick Hart (Kalamazoo, MI: Cistercian Publications, 1977). The title was reissued by Cistercian Publications in 1992. The essay itself was later printed as a small book illustrated by Merton's photos: Thomas Merton, *Basic Principles of Monastic Spirituality* (Springfield, IL: Templegate Publishers, 1996), 7. Subsequent references herein are to the Templegate edition as *Basic Principles*.

monastic life can only be seen in the light of the mystery of Christ. Christ is the center of monastic living. He is its source and its end. He is the way of the monk as well as his goal."[2]

The monastic life and its spirituality begin with a relationship to Jesus Christ. In his book *Strangers to the City: Reflections on the Beliefs and Values of the Rule of Saint Benedict*, the Australian Cistercian Dom Michael Casey writes, "Christianity defines self-realization in terms of relationship with God. We also affirm that the 'way' or 'road' by which human fulfillment is obtained is a dynamic and deepening personal relationship to Jesus."[3] Casey believes that the monastic vocation begins and continues via this relationship to Jesus. "Monastic life presupposes all sorts of external observances and deprivations, but these are secondary. What drives them is an untrammeled interior affectivity that has its focus on the person of Christ."[4] Monastic spirituality is the spirituality of the lovers of Christ.

2. *Basic Principles*, 7. And see Bonnie Thurston, " 'An Entirely New Spiritual Reality': Thomas Merton on Life in Christ," *The Merton Annual* 27 (2014): 122–32.

3. Michael Casey, *Strangers to the City* (Brewster, MA: Paraclete Press, 2013/2018), 145.

4. Casey, *Strangers*, 149. And see chapter 10 of his book, "Christ."

The first question Benedict asks of a prospective monk has to do with basic motivation: "Friend, for what purpose have you come?" (RB 60.3). I am put in mind of Jesus' questions to the disciples of John the Baptist: "What are you looking for?" (John 1:38) and to those who come to Gethsemane to arrest him; "Friend, why are you here?" (Matt 26:50, RSV) is Jesus' question to Judas, and "Whom do you seek?" is the question Jesus asks the arresting soldiers in John 18:4. These questions seek to discern fundamental motives. The Latin question *Quid petis?* (For what do you seek?) is part of the liturgy by which a monk becomes a monk. For Merton, the "what" is a "whom." He says monks "seek Jesus not only as our personal, individual salvation, but as the salvation and the unity of all. . . . We cannot fully understand this," he notes, "if we do not understand the love and compassion of Christ in our weakness."[5]

Looking back on his monastic beginnings, Merton confesses that they are Christological. The story starts with Jesus. The narrative of Merton's monastic life and the spirituality it espouses is the story of Christ's love and compassion to him, to his monastic brothers and sisters, and to the whole world. While it may sound a bit hokey, Merton's understanding of monastic (and Christian) spiritual life comes from his own experience:

5. *Basic Principles*, 49.

he once was lost but then was found, was blind but then he saw. And then, importantly, he shared what he saw in some of the most honest, eloquent, and engaging spiritual writing of the late twentieth century. He was, as Lawrence Cunningham so succinctly put it, a "spiritual master" and one whose spirituality was fundamentally monastic, and from that taproot grew its universal appeal.[6] Merton was a spiritual master who was a devoted disciple of the Master. He was not a perfected human being, nor did he attempt to present himself as such, and this is part of his appeal to many readers.

This book is not a biography of Merton but a study of his spiritual vision and practice and how both are important for Christian growth and maturity both inside and beyond the monastery. Several excellent biographies exist. I recommend some that I prefer in the reading suggestions at the end of this book. To appreciate Merton's monastic spirituality, we need to have some understanding of how he became a monk, and that is what this chapter seeks to provide in very skeletal form. If you want the complete story, read Merton's still riveting 1948 autobiography *The Seven Storey Mountain*, but do bear in mind it was written when he was still a

6. Lawrence S. Cunningham, ed., *Thomas Merton: Spiritual Master, The Essential Writings* (New York: Paulist Press, 1992). In *Thomas Merton and the Monastic Vision* (Grand Rapids, MI: Eerdmans, 1999) Cunningham also makes the convincing case that Merton's vision was essentially monastic.

very young man and is certainly not his final word. It is the story of the origin of his life in the Word.

From the beginning of my study of Merton (now some forty years ago), Merton's biography has struck me as a metaphor for, or a template of, modern life in at least three ways. It was rootless, privileged, and ripe for conversion. First, it was *rootless*. Merton was born in 1915 while his parents lived in Prades, France. They moved to his mother's home in Douglaston, Long Island, New York, in the United States in 1916 to escape the war. His mother died there of stomach cancer in 1921, and the effects of this on Merton cannot be overestimated. Leaving his brother, John Paul, Merton went with his artist father to Bermuda in 1922, then to St. Antonin, France, in 1925, from which he was sent to public school in England in 1928, first to Ripley Court and then to Oakham in 1929. Merton was orphaned at the age of sixteen, when his father died in 1931 of brain cancer. He subsequently graduated from Oakham School with a scholarship to Clare College, Cambridge, to read Modern Languages but (like more than one first-year collegian) made such a hash of his first year that he was summoned back to the United States by his maternal grandfather in 1934. He enrolled in Columbia University, had a roaring good time, achieved academic success, made important lifelong friends, and underwent a serious spiritual awakening.

Merton's was an ungrounded childhood and adolescence, but one of *privilege*. He was well provided for financially, educated at excellent schools in the United

Kingdom and the United States. During his years as a late adolescent and young adult, he traveled extensively in Europe (as National Socialism was consuming Germany). He was shaped by the artistic sensibilities of his parents, both artists, his father a painter of note. From childhood he was in contact with levels of culture unknown by many of his American contemporaries, and he himself was artistically gifted, not only as a writer, but as a calligrapher, artist, and photographer. I could make the case that his intellectual development and cultural outlook were distinctly European and not American. He did not become an American citizen until 1951. In any case, Michael Casey remarks that "Merton was a man of high culture, with an acute aesthetic sensibility and a gift for language."[7]

Finally, like many in the mid-century and after the Second World War, Merton was ripe for *conversion*. He had never had a steady, guiding hand or sense of purpose. Although he admired the piety of a French Catholic family with whom he briefly boarded, he had received only cursory religious instruction largely at English public schools of which he wrote unflatteringly in *The Seven Storey Mountain*, especially in part 1, chapter 3, titled "The Harrowing of Hell." As noted, he made a mess of his first year at Cambridge, was summoned to return to the United States, where he enrolled in Columbia in New

7. Michael Casey, "Thomas Merton and Monastic Renewal," *Cistercian Studies Quarterly* 53, no. 2 (2018): 184.

York City and, by his own admission, played the role of "big man on campus." Very little in his life, except perhaps with the exception of spiritual experiences in Rome in 1933[8] (in chapter 6 of "The Harrowing of Hell"), which was by his own admission frivolous and dissipated, foreshadowed his Christian conversion and monastic life. (My experience of monastics is that something similar is true of any number of them, but I shall not name names.)

The old saw is correct: God does work in mysterious ways. Merton read literature at Columbia and took a BA (1937) and an MA (1938), both in English, and, as many English majors (including this one) have been, he was introduced to Christian theology and the interior life of Christian spirituality by the great writers in the English tradition, in his case especially the metaphysical poets (John Donne, George Herbert, Henry Vaughn, Richard Crashaw), William Blake (about whom he wrote his MA thesis), and Gerard Manley Hopkins (whom he was studying at the time of his conversion). In 1937 he (almost mistakenly) bought a copy of Etienne Gilson's *The Spirit of Medieval Philosophy*, which he saw in a bookshop window. It was, he said, providential and helped to shape and direct his vocation.[9]

8. I am grateful to Professor Patrick O'Connell for reminding me of this episode in Merton's life.

9. See Merton's extended reflection on the effect of the book in *The Seven Storey Mountain* (Garden City, NY: Doubleday/Image, 1970), part 2, chapter 1.

He took Daniel Walsh's class on Aquinas and Duns Scotus and pursued his interest in Roman Catholicism under the influence of Walsh and of the poet Mark Van Doren, both Columbia professors. He met a Hindu monk, Bramachari, and when Merton asked him for suggestions for spiritual reading, the Hindu said he should read Christian classics like Augustine's *Confessions* and *The Imitation of Christ*. While reading a life of Hopkins (can we attribute Merton's decision for Christianity to that earlier convert priest/poet?) Merton reports,

> something began to stir within me, something began to push me, to prompt me. It was a movement that spoke like a voice.
>
> "What are you waiting for? . . . Why don't you do it?"

He walked the nine blocks to 121st Street, knocked on the door, and asked to see the priest. "Father, I want to become a Catholic."[10] He was baptized a Roman Catholic Christian in Corpus Christi Church, New York City, on November 16, 1938.

That was the beginning of what became the monastic story. Merton, who was already on the way to being a writer, then had to sort out his *Christian* vocation. He considered moving to Harlem to assist Baron-

10. Merton, *The Seven Storey Mountain*, 262 and 263.

ess de Hueck in whose work he volunteered. He applied for postulancy with the Franciscans and was turned down for being a bit too frank about his earlier life. (I often wonder what became of that Franciscan novice master.) Having finished his MA, he taught English at St. Bonaventure (then) College, Olean, New York, in 1940 and 1941 and was encouraged by Daniel Walsh to make a retreat at the Abbey of Our Lady of Gethsemani in Kentucky in the spring of 1941. That retreat shifted the tectonic plates of his life.

He returned from it to St. Bonaventure and began to pray in earnest about his vocation, this time to monastic life. While praying on the college grounds he records,

> I became aware of the wood, the trees, the dark hills, the wet night wind, and then, clearer than any of the obvious realities, in my imagination, I started to hear the great bell of Gethsemani ringing in the night. . . . I had to think twice to realize that it was only in my imagination that I was hearing the bell of the Trappist Abbey ringing in the dark. . . . It was just about that time that the bell is rung every night for the Salve Regina. . . .
>
> The bell seemed to be telling me where I belonged—as if it were calling me home.[11]

11. *The Seven Storey Mountain*, 441–42.

Merton, the privileged orphan boy, the well-educated European, the American man about town, was called to monastic life. As all Trappist monasteries are dedicated to Our Lady, and the bell he heard was, he later recalled, for the *Salve Regina* that then closed Compline in every Cistercian abbey, I think that she herself was involved in his vocation and took him as her son. (He later says as much in several contexts.) Certainly he had a deep devotion to Mary for his whole life. Many think the long poem *Hagia Sophia* is his best, and his devotion to Mary is beautifully illustrated in Jonathan Montaldo's collection of Merton's prayers and drawings, *Dialogues with Silence*.[12] In Merton's possession when he died were a Timex watch, a broken rosary, and a small icon of the Virgin and Child.

In the first week of December 1941, two letters arrived at St. Bonaventure for Merton, one from Gethsemani and one from the Draft Board.[13] December 7,

12. Thomas Merton, *Dialogues with Silence*, ed. Jonathan Montaldo (San Francisco, CA: HarperSanFrancisco, 2001).

13. I have heard people speculate that it was *convenient* to enter the monastery just after having received and responded to a draft notice. But, in fact, he couldn't at that point be drafted because he didn't have enough teeth to meet draft requirements. This is what happens to a boy who doesn't have a mother to make him brush his teeth!

Patrick O'Connell reminded me that Merton had decided to go to Gethsemani before Pearl Harbor and before he received the letter from the draft board.

1941: Pearl Harbor. December 10, 1941: Merton arrived at the Abbey of Gethsemani and entered as a postulant on St. Lucy's Day, December 13, 1941. He took solemn vows in 1947, and the next year the story of how he got to Our Lady of Gethsemani in rural Kentucky was published to great acclaim and astonishing commercial success. *The Seven Storey Mountain* is taking its place among the great Christian spiritual autobiographies. Merton was ordained priest in 1949. From 1951 to 1955 he was master of scholastics (monks studying to be priests), and from 1955 to 1965, master of novices. Happily, as part of the Monastic Wisdom Series, and under the brilliant and exacting editorship of Patrick F. O'Connell, Liturgical Press has published numerous volumes of his notes and lectures to these groups. (See the bibliography at the end of this book.) With very few, brief exceptions, Merton remained at Gethsemani until the autumn of 1968, when Abbot Flavian Burns granted permission for a monastic pilgrimage to Asia. In Bangkok, on December 10, 1968, after giving a talk to superiors of Asian religious communities, Merton died of accidental electrocution.[14]

14. Rumors that Merton's death was not accidental, that he was a victim of the CIA or some other nefarious group, have circulated for years. There is absolutely no hard evidence for this. I have read the accounts of those who first examined the body (and I have seen pictures of the corpse), including that of one of the abbesses at the meeting who was also a medical doctor. An ungrounded fan was

From the extraordinary autobiography written by a very young man and relatively new monk to the now sometimes cringeworthy hagiographical works written under obedience in his early monastic life, throughout his monastic life Merton was a prolific writer in many genres: novels (only one was published), a play, poetry (*The Collected Poems* runs to over one thousand pages), literary criticism,[15] social analysis, devotional and spiritual works, monastic history, and now seven volumes of his complete journals and five volumes of his collected letters. The sheer volume of his output is staggering. He was a seminal thinker in what I consider the three most important religious issues of the mid-twentieth century: ecumenism and interreligious dialogue, social justice (which includes the issues of peace, nuclear war, racism, and, as Monica Weis has demonstrated, ecology[16]), and contemplative spirituality. The reintroduction of contemplative prayer (or the "prayer of quiet") into Western Christianity in the United States, its subsequent avail-

---

found across his body. Either he had a heart attack and fell against the fan or touched it and was electrocuted. Anyone who has lived in the less developed world will attest to, if not undependable electricity, at least "adventures" with electricity. Merton scholar and journalist Robert Grip has done extensive work on this issue and concludes the death was accidental.

15. See *The Literary Essays of Thomas Merton*, ed. Patrick Hart (New York: New Directions, 1981).

16. Monica Weis, *The Environmental Vision of Thomas Merton* (Lexington: University Press of Kentucky, 2011).

ability to all Christians, not just monastics and religious, is traceable directly to the writings of Thomas Merton. Now, fifty years after his death, there are major secondary studies on his thought in all of these categories, and he continues to shape our discussion on these matters into this century. But, first and foremost, the man who had such insightful things to say about so many important issues was a monk, and, happily, there are several excellent books that focus on Merton the monk.[17] The subject of this book is how Merton understood some aspects of the monastic spirituality that undergirded all the rest of his thought and work.

The trajectory of Merton's life is not unfamiliar to us. We know the pattern from Augustine's *Confessions*, from the writings of St. Gregory the Great, and from William James's classic work on religious experience. The traditional pattern is as follows: Worldly living and often sensual extravagance precede an insight in which the nugatory quality of mundane things and the sublime value of the spiritual life are recognized. After this

17. See, for example, John Eudes Bamberger, *Thomas Merton: Prophet of Renewal*, Monastic Wisdom 4 (Collegeville, MN: Cistercian Publications, 2005); Lawrence S. Cunningham, *Thomas Merton and the Monastic Vision*; Patrick Hart, ed., *Survival or Prophecy? The Letters of Thomas Merton and Jean Leclercq* (New York: Farrar, Straus & Giroux, 2002); Patrick Hart, *Thomas Merton, Monk: A Monastic Tribute* (New York: Sheed & Ward, 1974; enlarged edition, Cistercian Studies 52, Kalamazoo, MI: Cistercian Publications, 1983).

initial glimpse of truth, the "pilgrim" begins a process of detachment from the corrupt world (*via purgativa*) and repudiation of the corrupt self (*contemptus sui*). This is basically a process of repentance and atonement that can be (but is not always) "rewarded" (a rather crass idea, to be sure) by the gift of a spiritual love that energizes the now new person and can (but does not always) lead to union with God (*theoria*). To put the process in more modern terms, a person escapes the inauthentic identity (what Merton calls the "False Self") in order to actualize the authentic one (Merton's "True Self").[18]

Somehow it always surprises us when God chooses unlikely persons for spiritual graces: like Jesus choosing Peter the impetuous fisherman and Simon the Zealot (a terrorist?) and Zacchaeus and all the unlikely beloved God has chosen through the ages. Merton, like Augustine, was able to articulate the process of his ongoing *metanoia* (change of heart; change of ways or direction), the *conversio morum*, the conversion of life that monastic life is organized to facilitate. His conversion was an interesting "hybrid" of William James's two basic forms of conversion, the volitional (conscious, voluntary, gradual) and the self-surrender (unconscious, sudden,

18. The concepts of the False and True Selves are perhaps most clearly set out by Merton in *New Seeds of Contemplation* (New York: New Directions, 1961), chapters 4–7. And see chapter 3 of this book.

perhaps as the result of a crisis).[19] He found his way by active searching, was directed to Christian monasticism by means of his own need, his openness to what Michael Casey aptly terms the "meta-experiential," and he was directed there by teachers and friends and by the mystery of a bell ringing in the night. As Merton wrote in *New Seeds of Contemplation*, "Our discovery of God is, in a way, God's discovery of us." God "comes down from heaven and finds us."[20]

James suggests the "proof" of conversion is that one's life is observably different to outsiders and that the converted person senses a "higher control" and experiences a "state of assurance," a sense that all is ultimately well, an ongoing perception of truths not known before, and an "objective change which the world appears to undergo. 'An appearance of newness beautifies every object.' "[21] One finds all this and more in Merton's prodigious writings. His autobiographical works in particular reveal a life that "turned from" rootlessness to stability, from privilege to poverty, from being lost to being found, a recognition of his belovedness. Merton

19. See William James's *The Varieties of Religious Experience* (New York: Collier 1961/1974), which originated in the Gifford Lectures at the University of Edinburgh in 1902, especially Lectures 9 and 10 on conversion.

20. Merton, *New Seeds*, 39.

21. James, *The Varieties of Religious Experience*, 202.

experienced "the love and compassion of Christ in his weakness" and understood himself as a man saved by Christ *from* himself and the world and, paradoxically perhaps, *for* the world.

In December 1941, Merton began to live the monastic life, began to allow its bud to flower in him. He wrote in *Thoughts in Solitude*, "A man knows when he has found his vocation when he stops thinking about how to live and begins to live."[22] "Life reveals itself to us," he explained, "only in so far as we live it."[23] As Merton lived into the monastic life, it revealed more of itself to him. His vocation may have begun as a *fuga mundi*, a flight from a world already rapidly disintegrating into war, but it developed as a gift *for* the world. The monastic vocation is never for the monk alone but for the Church and the world in which it either withers or flourishes. Merton's monastic vocation was a gift both to him and, through him, to the world, to us, which is why it seems important to investigate something of what he says about the spirituality that drew, embraced, nurtured, and revealed to him the person God created him to be.

22. Thomas Merton, *Thoughts in Solitude* (New York: Noonday/Farrar, Straus & Giroux, 1956/1977), 87.

23. Merton, *Thoughts in Solitude*, 57.

Chapter 2

The Temptation of "Holier Than Thou"

Almost from its beginnings Christianity has opined that there are two categories of Christians. There are we ordinary, run-of-the-mill Christians doing the best we can in "the world." And there are the spiritual elite, those who have a special calling, the priests and monks and nuns and religious. The unspoken but clear assumption has been that they are God's favorites, the ecclesial and spiritual equivalent of "Dad loves us both, but he loves me more than he loves you."

I don't believe this for a moment. It is a simplistic overstatement, one that for a time Vatican II, which clearly pointed out its shortcomings, helped the Church move away from. Yet we sometimes catch a whiff of it in writing about monastic life and theology, those popular "monastic practices for non-monks" books.[1] It's odd

---

1. I'm thinking of books like the wildly popular *The Cloister Walk* by Kathleen Norris (New York: Riverhead, 1996) or the now classic

how often we seem to want something other than what
we have. If we have curly hair, we want straight hair; if
straight, we want curly. If we are too tall, we want to
be shorter, and vice versa. The longing to be something
other than what we are occurs in spite of the fact that
God made us as we are for God's purposes. We are as
God made us. Paul articulated this clearly and wrote
to the Ephesian Christians, "[W]e are what [God] has
made us, created in Christ Jesus for good works, which
God created beforehand to be our way of life" (Eph
2:10). Some nonmonastics long for monastic life (or
think they do). Some of them do have genuine vocations, and it's important to discern whether the inclina-
tion is genuine or of the "grass is always greener on the
other side" variety. And, I've known some monastics
who eventually wanted a "get out of jail free" card!

In his middle monastic years, Merton too felt the con-
strictions of the life he had chosen. It seems to be a stage
in the developmental pattern of monastics, and perhaps
the rest of us, as well. (One still hears the old saw about
the "seven-year itch" in discussions of married life.) After

---

by Esther de Waal, *Seeking God: The Way of St. Benedict* (Collegeville,
MN: Liturgical Press, 1984) or Sr. Mary Margaret Funk's series of
books on monastic practices and attitudes (for example, *Thoughts
Matter, Humility Matters, Lectio Matters*) or the writings of Michael
Casey, recently *Strangers to the City* (Brewster, MA: Paraclete Press,
2013/2018). Paraclete Press, a ministry of the monastic Community of Jesus, has published several such books.

Merton's baptism in 1938, as the Europe in which he grew up was on the verge of war, he was sincerely looking for *how* to be Christian. After his first retreat at Gethsemani in 1941 he found his "way." He fell in love with monasticism and, as it often is after falling in love, there was an extended honeymoon period in which the beloved seemed perfect in every way. Within ten years, his writing indicated that the honeymoon was over.[2]

Monasticism and marriage have several things in common. Both, as Merton understood, are vocations. "We would be better able to understand," he wrote, "the beauty of the religious vocation if we remembered that marriage too is a vocation."[3] Another commonality between the two is that after we take vows, we face the reality of, and live into, the love we have chosen and that has chosen us. It is easy to forget that, in both states of life, we have responded to being chosen, and we have chosen. This life isn't "someone else's fault." What Merton wrote of monasticism in his essay "The Monastic Renewal: Problems and Prospects" is profoundly true of both states of life: "The true strength of monasticism is to be sought in its capacity for renunciation, silence, prayer, faith, and its realization of the

2. Peruse, for example, *A Search for Solitude*, The Journals of Thomas Merton, vol. 3: *1952–1960*, ed. Lawrence S. Cunningham (San Francisco: HarperSanFrancisco, 1996).

3. Thomas Merton, *No Man Is an Island* (New York: Doubleday, Image, 1955/1967), 121.

cross in our lives."[4] And, of course, as Charles de Foucauld (whose own spirituality was shaped by his years as a Trappist) taught, "The more firmly we embrace the cross, the more closely we are bound to Jesus, our Beloved, who is made fast to it."[5]

Monastic spirituality takes as its model and goal the carpenter (*tekton*, literally the "builder" or "skilled craftsman") from Nazareth, the One who apparently lived an ordinary village life for most of his thirty-some years. Christian life, and monastic life in particular, is to approximate the life of one who was so humble that we know almost nothing about that life before his baptism and public ministry. The gospels mostly pick up at that point and certainly are not modern, psychological biographies. They give only glimpses of Jesus' own developing self-understanding. The only thing he says directly about himself in the Synoptic Gospels is the "I am" of Matthew 11:29: "I am gentle and humble in heart." Monastic life involves a gentling and humbling of the human person. Its great temptation is to glory in itself. We see hints of that temptation in Merton's own monastic experience.

Interestingly, in view of the fact that there are seven volumes of Merton's journals, almost nothing remains

4. Thomas Merton, "The Monastic Renewal: Problems and Prospects," in *Thomas Merton: Selected Essays*, ed. Patrick F. O'Connell (Maryknoll, NY: Orbis Books, 2013), 388.

5. Robert Ellsberg, ed., *Charles de Foucauld*, Modern Spiritual Masters Series (Maryknoll, NY: Orbis Books, 1999), 127.

of his first monastic journals but drafts of some poems. Those early poems give glimpses of Merton's earliest monastic life.[6] I think they depict the big temptation of a monastic vocation: to assume one is specially favored by it, to assume it sets one apart from the rest of humanity as a different sort of person with all the attendant difficulties of that attitude. Traditional Christian writing calls this attitude "pride" or "vainglory" (frequently translated "conceit," the Greek word literally means "empty glory"[7]), and sincere and serious Christians are subject to it and warned against it. It is a great temptation or danger for those who have walked some little distance along the spiritual path and why so many find potholes in or obstructions on the path. That point of temptation may be a particular grace in that it calls one back to herself and to the model of Christ. It is exactly as Bernardo Bonowitz suggested in a retreat he gave for the Merton Centenary: "What saves the monk, if he is truly seeking God . . . is the experience of failure, failure that comes through the divinely conceded gift of self-knowledge."[8]

6. For an excellent exposition of these early years, see Patrick F. O'Connell, "Trappists, Working—Trappists Praying: The Earliest Monastic Poetry of Thomas Merton," *The Merton Annual* 29 (2016): 99–124.

7. *Kenodoxia*; see Philippians 2:3.

8. Bernardo Bonowitz, "Reaping Where Merton Has Sown: A Retreat for the Merton Centenary," *Cistercian Studies Quarterly* 50, no. 1 (2015): 56.

Merton entered at Gethsemani as a postulant on St. Lucy's Day, December 13, 1941. I love this little fact that he entered on the day of the saint who is depicted with a crown of candles, a halo of light on one of the darkest days of the year. His journal entry for that day is "Poem for My Friends, December 12–13" published as "A Letter to My Friends on Entering the Monastery of Our Lady of Gethsemani, 1941," which first appeared in the collection *A Man in the Divided Sea*, 1946. In the poem, Gethsemani, "This holy House of God," is compared to Nazareth, the place of the hidden life of Jesus. It is the place "Where separate strangers, hid in their disguises, / Have come to meet by night, the quiet Christ."[9] (This, it seems to me, provides an attractive, functional definition of a monastery.) In the poem, Merton looks back at the world he left behind and calls it "ruins," "sad towns," "sick cities" as opposed to his chosen "holy desert" and "holy hill." "Where fields are the friends of plenteous heaven, / Where starlight feeds, as bright as manna, / All our rough earth with wakeful grace." The whole poem is a kind of love letter to the Abbey of Our Lady of Gethsemani.

9. References to the poem are from *The Collected Poems of Thomas Merton* (New York: New Directions, 1977), 90–92. Canadian professor Lynn R. Szabo has done a splendid selection of Merton's poems, *In the Dark Before Dawn: New Selected Poems of Thomas Merton* (New York: New Directions, 2005). I highly recommend it.

Separated from friends in New York City, Merton writes them a letter in the form of a poem that compares the hidden life of Christ with the hidden life of a monk in rural Kentucky. The world he left was in bad shape. The world he entered was the House of God, the new Jerusalem. Except it didn't quite turn out that way. Merton discovered (I know you will be deeply shocked to learn this) that monasteries are full of imperfect people and imperfect systems. Like the old desert Christians of the fourth century, Merton fled from a very literally disintegrating world to the relative safety of monastic life. But he hadn't quite yet grasped that the monastic vocation is not for the individual alone but for the whole Church and the whole world. A genuine monastic is not separated *from* but in solidarity *with*, and this is true for serious Christians in any state of life. (The following chapter will expand on this point.)

Another manifestation of Merton's "big temptation" was to think himself different from his brother monks. Volume 3 of his journals, which cover the years from 1952 to 1960, is a long screed on how mistreated he is. (And see note 2 and part 5 of Michael Mott's massive biography.[10]) I have had the joy of knowing some of Merton's brothers and knew his last abbot, so I know that there was perhaps never a Trappist for whom

10. Michael Mott, *The Seven Mountains of Thomas Merton* (Boston: Houghton Mifflin, 1984).

more breaks were cut and more exceptions made. In the 1950s and early 1960s, however, Merton was exploring other monastic options. Perhaps this is a normal stage of monastic development, and, if so, it is one conducted on spiritual thin ice in view of the Benedictine and Trappist vow of stability. One vows oneself to the Life itself, in the same place and with the same people, for life. As Esther de Waal observed in the chapter on stability in her classic book *Seeking God: The Way of St. Benedict*, "The stability of space and of relationships are all the means towards the establishment of stability of the heart."[11]

Merton's poem "The Reader," which appeared in his 1949 collection *The Tears of the Blind Lions*, perhaps unbeknownst to Merton, reflects a certain separation from other monks. The reader is a monastic who serves the community by reading to it at silent meals.[12] The poem is cast in first person, "I." The reader "Waiting for the monks to come" has "won light to read by." As his brother monks "pause upon the step," the reader is "here in this lectern," standing, perhaps above them. "My tongue," he says, not *our* tongue, "shall sing Thy Scripture."[13]

---

11. de Waal, *Seeking God*, 60.
12. See The Rule of St. Benedict, chapter 38.
13. Quotations from Merton, *Collected Poems*, 74–75.

The Reader

Lord, when the clock strikes
Telling the time with cold tin
And I sit hooded in this lectern

Waiting for the monks to come,
I see the red cheeses, and bowls
All smile with milk in ranks upon their tables.

Light fills my proper globe
(I have won light to read by
With a little, tinkling chain)

And the monks come down the cloister
With robes as voluble as water.
I do not see them, but I hear their waves.

It is winter, and my hands prepare
To turn the pages of the saints:
And to the trees Thy moon has frozen on the
    windows
My tongue shall sing Thy Scripture.

Then the monks pause upon the step
(With me here in this lectern
And Thee there on Thy crucifix)
And gather little pearls of water on their fingers' ends
Smaller than this my psalm.[14]

14. *Collected Poems*, 202–3. Used with permission.

It is a lovely poem, full of striking, sensual images. The overall picture doesn't reflect great *koinonia*, however, but is of the reader as separate from those to whom he reads and, if it reflects reality, is potentially a dangerous one in a cenobitic community.

Fast forward about ten years to March 18, 1958. Merton was in Louisville, Kentucky, when he had the "Fourth and Walnut" epiphany that Christine Bochen rightly notes "symbolized a turning point in his self-understanding."[15] He recorded the experience in his journal and then expanded it to be included in *Conjectures of a Guilty Bystander*, published in 1966. Here is the 1958 journal entry:

> Yesterday, in Louisville, at the corner of 4th . . . [a]nd Walnut, suddenly realized that I loved all the people and that none of them were, or, could be totally alien to me. As if waking from a dream—the dream of my separateness, of the "special" vocation to be different. My vocation does not really make me different from the rest of men or put me in a special category except artificially, juridically. I am still a member of the human race—and what more glorious destiny is there . . . since the Word was made flesh and became, too, a member of the Human Race!

15. Christine M. Bochen, ed., *Thomas Merton: Essential Writings* (Maryknoll, NY: Orbis Books, 2000), 90. There is a substantial secondary literature on the Fourth and Walnut event.

Thank God! Thank God! I am only another member
of the human race, like all the rest of them.[16]

The journal entry goes on to describe his reaction to the
women he sees on the street in relation to his vow of
chastity, his focused interest in Wisdom, and "Proverb,"
the dream figure who represents his *anima* and appears
with some frequency in his writing. Merton scholars
note that it was *after* this epiphany of his humanness,
his understanding he is "another member of the human
race, like all the rest," his recognition of sameness and
solidarity with ordinary people, that he turned seriously
to engagement with social issues like racism, war, and
nuclear proliferation.

Fast forward once more to May 1965 when Merton
wrote *Day of a Stranger* in response to the request of a
South American editor for a description of his life in the
hermitage on the grounds of Gethsemani to which he
moved that year. In it he declares, "What I wear is pants.
What I do is live. How I pray is breathe."[17] In other

16. Merton, *A Search for Solitude*, 181–82.
17. Thomas Merton, *Day of a Stranger* (Salt Lake City: Gibbs
M. Smith, Inc., 1981), 41. This edition is illustrated with Merton's
photographs. Versions of the text also appear in a section of *Dancing in the Water of Life*, The Journals of Thomas Merton, vol. 5:
1963–1965, ed. Robert E. Daggy (San Francisco: HarperSanFrancisco, 1997), 239–42, and in *Thomas Merton: Selected Essays* (see
note 4), 232–39.

words, "I'm just a regular guy." Of the essay Patrick O'Connell writes, "He is a 'stranger' not because he lives an exotic existence apart from others, but only in the sense that he is aware that his identity, like that of everyone, is a mystery that cannot be defined by a role or a function."[18] He is as God made him. Period.

Merton's monastic development involved a serious spiritual temptation. His early life was at best a muddle. Christ found him, and he responded not only in submitting to baptism, but to giving his life fully to Christ by accepting his monastic vocation. The lintel over the great gate at Gethsemani reads, "For God Alone."[19] Merton left a corrupt world for a perfect monastery that turned out to be, like everything else temporal, not so perfect. He was specially called and separated himself from the world and may well have been tempted to think of himself as special among his brothers. I use the conditional form because we can know another's motivation only when he directly tells us what it is. As the Psalmist wrote: God "knows the secrets of the heart" (Ps 44:21). I don't know what Merton thought unless he recorded it and certainly not "what he would have done" had he lived beyond the 1960s. Then, on

18. O'Connell, *Selected Essays*, 233.

19. Michael Casey reports, "The only monastery I know where this is true is Gethsemani." "Thomas Merton and Monastic Renewal," *Cistercian Studies Quarterly* 53, no. 2 (2018): 164, note 28.

an ordinary day in an ordinary place *not* the monastery, the monk who had been in solemn vows ten years was given a vision of the unity of humanity, our oneness, our connectedness to everyone and everything else.

The monastic way can transform and make one more humble and Christ-like, but it does not *necessarily* make one "holier than thou," holier than ordinary people on an ordinary street on an ordinary day doing ordinary things. In a notebook of May 1968 Merton wrote, "A role is not necessarily a vocation. One can be alienated by role filling."[20] And this is especially true, as Merton's later writing on monastic life and renewal asserts, if one must conform him- or herself to someone else's rigid definition of the "role." A vocation is a living thing and, like all living things, must grow and change or face an early demise. To quote Ruth Burrows, OCD, "To take for granted we are further advanced than we are ends our progress."[21] It also reflects a lack of humility.

Monastic life holds in tension several paradoxes. The gift of a monastic vocation *is* a special gift. Not all are so called. But it is *not* an invitation to a personal sense of "specialness" or "uniqueness" if that excludes or separates one from others. That way lays the ur-sin of *hubris*,

20. Thomas Merton, *Woods, Shore, Desert* (Santa Fe: Museum of New Mexico Press, 1982), 5.

21. Ruth Burrows, *Guidelines for Mystical Prayer* (New York: Paulist Press, 2017), 60.

of pride. St. Benedict suggested obedience and humility were the basic monastic virtues. He opens chapter 7 of the Rule (Humility) by quoting Luke 14:11 and 18:14 in which Jesus says the exalted will be humbled and the humble will be exalted (which, of course, echoes a basic idea in Mary his mother's *Magnificat*). Benedict continues by saying that monks attain heaven by means of the ladder of humility: "[W]e descend by exaltation and ascend by humility."[22] In the published version of Merton's conferences to novices on the Rule of St. Benedict, some sixty-four pages are devoted to humility.[23] More recently, Sr. Mary Margaret Funk, OSB, has devoted a book to the importance of humility. It opens, "Humility matters. . . . [T]he root of most of the anguish on earth is the human ego in denial of its true vocation: to renounce our false self and to embrace our baptismal initiation into Christ Jesus."[24] She continues, "[H]umility is the unmistakable character of one who has accepted the vocation to take the spiritual journey."[25]

22. Timothy Fry, *The Rule of St. Benedict* (Collegeville, MN: Liturgical Press, 1981), 193.

23. Thomas Merton, *The Rule of St. Benedict: Initiation into the Monastic Tradition 4*, ed. Patrick F. O'Connell (Collegeville, MN: Cistercian Publications, 2009).

24. Mary Margaret Funk, *Humility Matters for Practicing the Spiritual Life* (New York: Continuum, 2005), 9.

25. Funk, *Humility Matters*, 10.

Returning to an image I used at the outset of this chapter, God is like a good parent who loves the children *equally* but *differently*. God's love for each of us is exquisitely individualized, as defining as a fingerprint or one's DNA. We are "fearfully and wonderfully made" (Ps 139:14), but made *differently,* so our callings are different. "Different" isn't a comparative category, not better or worse than. We are, indeed, "what [God] has made us," with gifts and weaknesses to fulfill *God's* purposes for our lives. Paul's explanation of spiritual gifts in 1 Corinthians 12–14 is a good gloss. Its principle is "To each is given the manifestation of the Spirit for the common good" (1 Cor 12:7). Merton learned in the course of his monastic life that a particular calling or *charism* doesn't make one any better than or ontologically different from anyone else. And it is precisely in the monastery (or in a healthy family) where this reality can be lived out.

Merton wrote in *Basic Principles of Monastic Spirituality*, "The Benedictine ascesis of silence, obedience, solitude, humility, manual labor, liturgical prayer, is all designed to unite us with the Mystical Christ, *with one another in charity*" (italics mine).[26] Monastic life and its spirituality are to unite, not separate, to foster deep commonality and mutual love among the "characters"

26. Thomas Merton, *Basic Principles of Monastic Spirituality* (Springfield, IL: Templegate, 1996), 66–67.

who populate monastic houses and for all those beyond the cloister. "God speaks, and God is to be heard," Merton wrote, "not only on Sinai, not only in my own heart, but in the *voice of the stranger*. . . . We must find [God] in our enemy, or we may lose him even in our friend" (italics in the original).[27]

Humility fosters self-transcendence, and self-transcendence almost always leads to deeper and more inclusive love, which Bernardo Bonowitz, OCSO, suggests Merton recognized as "the unique and universal vocation."[28] God infuses "his own love into the human heart by the outpouring of the Holy Spirit," and "this identifying of the human person with divine love itself leads to universal compassion."[29] If we seek to be united to the risen Christ, we will, whether we like it or not, be drawn to the whole human family—indeed, if we believe St. Paul, to the whole *creation*, for which Christ gave himself on the cross (see Rom 8:19-23). Writing in *Wisdom of the Desert*, Merton said, "Isolation in the self, inability to go out of oneself to others, would mean incapacity for any form of self-transcendence." He continues, "Love takes one's neighbor as one's other self, and loves him with . . . immense humility and

27. Letter to Pablo Antonio Cuadra in *Collected Poems*, 384.
28. Bonowitz, "Reaping Where Merton Has Sown," 57.
29. Bonowitz, 57.

discretion and reserve and reverence."[30] Monastic life has been, and always will be, about responding to a vocation, about the vows and the liturgy and the *lectio* and the labor . . . but greater than these is the love.

It was learning this life of commonality, of a common love for each other and their combined love for God, that was the taproot of Merton's concern for the world, a world in which nobody is "holier than thou" and everybody is the recipient of the grace and love of a most extraordinary Parent.

30. Thomas Merton, *The Wisdom of the Desert: Sayings from the Desert Fathers of the Fourth Century* (New York: New Directions, 1960), 17 and 18.

Chapter 3

Merton's Presuppositions

Thomas Merton entered the monastery as a writer and remained one during his whole monastic life. Many who have read *The Seven Storey Mountain* undoubtedly remember the passage in the epilogue when, as a young monk, Merton struggles with the dual vocations of writer/monk and describes the writer as a Judas who hides behind the pillars and disturbs his prayers with his whispers and, worst of all, Judas has his superiors on his side. Early on, Merton struggled to reconcile the vocations of writer and monk and wrote under obedience, by his own admission, some really awful stuff, as the graph he drew in 1967 evaluating his own books illustrates.[1]

---

1. The graph appears in *Introductions East and West: The Foreign Prefaces of Thomas Merton*, ed. Robert E. Daggy (Greensboro, NC: Unicorn Press, Inc., 1981), 126–27.

It is sublime understatement to say that Merton wrote a *lot* and, as you will remember from chapter 1, in many genres: novels, poetry, a play, letters (thousands of them), journals (seven published volumes), works of practical and monastic theology, spirituality, social and political critique. It is dizzying and suggests that if ever there were a modern monastic polymath, it was Thomas Merton, almost certainly history's talkiest Trappist.

As one traces his monastic life through his writing, one finds that his basic life stance moves from "knowing" to "being known," from being "speaker" to being "one spoken." By 1956 or so he could say of his relationship with God, "My life is a listening, [God's] is a speaking."[2] This attitude of listening is crucial not only to the monastic life but to growth in the spiritual life in general and to healthy human relationships. Most of us need to shut stuff off, shut up, and *listen*. In chapter 4 of Mark's gospel, the "parable chapter," Jesus four times commands "listen." St. Benedict opens the Rule: "Listen carefully . . . to the master's instructions, and attend to them with the ear of your heart."[3] What would it mean in a world that tends to be filled with "talkers" rather than "listeners" if there were a

2. Thomas Merton, *Thoughts in Solitude* (New York: Noonday/ Farrar, Straus & Giroux, 1956/1977), 74.

3. Timothy Fry, ed., *The Rule of St. Benedict* (Collegeville, MN: Liturgical Press, 1981), 157.

shift toward "listening with our hearts"? It would almost certainly mean that we would live in a quieter,
less fraught world.

Merton came to the realization that he didn't know
as much as he once thought he did. He opens *Conjectures of a Guilty Bystander*, a collection of reflections
taken largely from his journals, by saying, "I do not
have clear answers to current questions. I do have questions, and . . . I think a man is known better by his
questions than by his answers."[4] As a university professor I too came to understand that questions are more
important than answers because the way the question
is asked usually determines the answer that is found. As
Merton noted in *Conjectures*, it also reveals a great deal
about the one who asks the question. Asking questions
involves the vulnerability of admitting we don't know
everything, and for most people this is difficult.

All that having been said, by his writing, Merton
became a major spokesman for the three consuming
religious issues of the late twentieth century and into
the twenty-first. I remind you that I suggested they
were interfaith dialogue and ecumenism, social justice
(war, nuclear proliferation, civil rights, ecology), and
contemplative spirituality. To understand the origins of
Merton's thought on these issues, especially the last,

4. Thomas Merton, *Conjectures of a Guilty Bystander* (Garden
City, NY: Doubleday/Image, 1966/1968), 5.

I suggest three fundamental presuppositions that undergird what he says in various specific contexts. First, Merton reverses our usual way of knowing. Second, he articulates an important ontology, an understanding of the human person as exhibiting a True or False Self. Third, he believes monastic life is profoundly connected to "the world."

As an aside, I warn the reader that in introducing these three principles many quotations from Merton follow and many of them use masculine references for God and the term "man" to include men and women. This reflects usage during Merton's lifetime, and I sincerely hope it will not result in our missing important things he has to teach us. Shakespeare used archaic language too, and we are diminished if we miss his important insights because they are veiled in the English of another age.

Merton Reverses Our Usual Way of Knowing

Largely because of the educational structures in the Western world, most of us "know" from the outside in. That is to say, we are Cartesians. Whether we know it or not, we follow René Descartes: we presume that we think, therefore we are. We view things as "objects of knowledge" that we acquire. Our language reflects this: we "get" a mathematical principle or "acquire" an education or even "take" a nap. (Doesn't a nap actually "take" us?) We "take in" information from the world around us. Notice, please, how grasping and acquisitive these verbs are. This *might* be okay so long as it doesn't lead to our living reactively, that is, by responding primarily to external stimuli rather than from active choice, or tangle us up in our own egoistic thought processes. Unfortunately, it often does both.

Merton challenges us to live from the inside out rather than from the outside in, to choose rather than to react, to trust our own, best, interior intuitions. One of my teachers in energy work used to say, "The body *never* lies." And this is true, although Merton didn't mean only physical reaction when he turned Cartesian thinking upside down. His "inside out" approach developed in Merton the conviction that it was more important to *be* known than to know. In this he echoes St. Paul, whose thought so deeply influenced Merton's theology:[5] "Now I know only in part," Paul wrote to the church at Corinth, "then I will know fully, *even as I have been fully known*" (1 Cor 13:12, italics mine). It can be terrifying to be "fully known," all the dark corners, all the rats in the soul's cellar, all the partiality, imperfections, and wounds. But when we feel lonely or

---

5. See, for example, Andy Lord, "Pauline Roots of Thomas Merton's Theology," *Cistercian Studies Quarterly* 54, no. 2 (2019): 211–26, and Bonnie Thurston, "Thomas Merton and St. Paul," *The Merton Seasonal* 34, no. 1 (2009): 14–19.

forgotten or vulnerable it can be an immense comfort to remember that we have been already and eternally and fully known. And not only known but loved. As Ruth Burrows, OCD, notes, we fear entrusting ourselves to Love, but "God loves me, not because I am good but because he is good."[6]

In *Conjectures of a Guilty Bystander* Merton wrote in the context of a meditation on St. Anselm, "God's will is not a force that presses down on man from the outside. It works on man from within himself and from within the ontological core of his own freedom."[7] This is a philosophical way of saying something Merton said in *New Seeds of Contemplation*:

> Our discovery of God is . . . God's discovery of us. . . . He comes down from heaven and finds us. . . . We only know Him in so far as we are known by Him, and our contemplation of Him is a participation in His contemplation of Himself.
>
> We become contemplative when God discovers Himself in us.[8]

A now, alas, frequently forgotten contemporary of Merton's, Dag Hammarskjold, spoke similarly of his offer-

6. Ruth Burrows, *Guidelines for Mystical Prayer* (New York: Paulist Press, 1976/2017), 62.

7. Merton, *Conjectures*, 329.

8. Thomas Merton, *New Seeds of Contemplation* (New York: New Directions, 1961), 39.

ing of self, he " 'surrendered' to *be* what, in me, God gives of Himself to Himself" (italics in original).[9] An important reason Merton (and Hammarskjold) suggests we live from the inside out is precisely that God is not only found in creation, or "out there somewhere," but within us. We might listen within for God's voice. Indeed, this is one of the great challenges of monastic life.

Merton's Monastic Spirituality Is Based on His notion of the True and False Self[10]

Closely related to the importance of living from "the inside out" is Merton's notion of the True and False Self, an idea that has "caught on" and that I now read frequently in recent spiritual writing, sometimes attributed to Merton and sometimes passed off as the author's own. Merton suggests we have two developmental options: to be our True Self, the person God created us to be (with all our strengths and weaknesses), or to be a False Self, a collection of aggregates of the expectations and roles society (and even monastic life) assigns to us. The False Self is another example of living

9. Dag Hammarskjold, *Markings* (New York: Alfred A. Knopf, 1964), 96.

10. I explored the False and True Selves at greater length in the essay "Self and World: Thomas Merton on the Two Directions of the Spiritual Life," which appeared in *Cistercian Studies* 18, no. 2 (1983): 149–55.

from the outside in, and Madison Avenue uses it to sell us stuff. Want to see a collection of false selves? Have a look at women's magazines or magazines pitched to men and notice how much those images of the feminine or masculine depend on acquisition of things, buying, and consuming.[11]

Although it appears in many places in his work, perhaps Merton's clearest presentation of the True and False Selves occurs in *New Seeds of Contemplation*, chapters 5–7. There he writes, "Every one of us is shadowed by an illusory person: a false self." It "wants to exist outside the reach of God's will and God's love." And we "are not very good at recognizing illusions, least of all the ones we cherish about ourselves."[12] Here, in our egocentric desires, sin originates. On the other hand, our True Self "is hidden in the love and mercy of God,"[13] and we discover it by listening toward God who utters God's self in us. Merton asserts, "God utters me like a word containing a partial thought of Himself."[14] Imagine that every person you see is a partial thought

---

11. I am hiding in a footnote my favorite description of the world of fashion. It is spoken by the character Sandra in Penelope Lively's novel *Family Album* (New York: Viking, 2009): "a sort of lunatic circus, playing to an audience of turnip heads" (190).

12. Merton, *New Seeds*, 34.

13. Merton, *New Seeds*, 35.

14. Merton, *New Seeds*, 37.

of God.[15] How differently we would treat each other if we believed that.

Bishop Kallistos Ware articulates the concept of the True Self from an Orthodox perspective as follows: "Because we are each endowed with free will, we are all of us different; each is unique, and each expresses the Divine image in his or her distinctive and unrepeatable way." He continues, "The question of all questions that will be put by God to each one of us at the *Parousia*: Why did you not become your own true self?"[16] I once saw a bumper sticker that said, "Be yourself. Everyone else is taken." Huston Smith put the matter more elegantly: "*Someone* must fill each of our roles, and it might as well be us."[17] Merton described, perhaps rather abstractly, the process of finding the True Self in chapter 7 of *No Man Is an Island*: "[W]hat we are is to be sought in the invisible depths of our own being, not in our outward reflection in our own acts. We must find our

15. I paraphrase a similar thought by the sometime Trappist, Charles de Foucauld: "See everyone as Jesus and act accordingly."

16. Kallistos Ware, "How Do We Enter the Heart?," in *Paths to the Heart: Sufism and the Christian East*, ed. James S. Cutsinger (Louisville, KY: Fons Vitae Press, 2002), 17. For more on Merton and Orthodoxy and the Eastern Church, see Bernadette Dieker and Jonathan Montaldo, eds., *Merton and Hesychasm: The Prayer of the Heart* (Louisville, KY: Fons Vitae Press, 2003).

17. Huston Smith, "The Long Way Home," in Cutsinger, *Paths to the Heart*, 255.

real selves not in the froth stirred up by the impact of our being upon the beings around us, but in our own soul which is the principle of all our acts."[18]

Listening and interiority are essential to Merton's understanding of monastic and Christian spirituality. You will not be surprised to learn that we are most likely to find the word that God utters in us in silence and solitude. (Discussions of both appear later in this book.) Merton writes beautifully of both in his poems "In Silence" and "Song: If You Seek," which we shall consider later. This leads to the last of Merton's "undergirding presuppositions" that I will lift up.

Monastic Life Is Profoundly Connected to "the World"

Monastic life, and more generally contemplative life, the life of prayer, is not, as is frequently imagined, a withdrawal from the world but a profound way of connecting with it, engaging on its behalf. The next chapter is devoted to the connections between contemplative life and our problem-laden world. For the moment, let me suggest that Merton understood that

18. Thomas Merton, *No Man Is an Island* (New York: Doubleday/Image 1955/1967), 97. For excellent exposition of the True and False Self in the context of Merton's understanding of contemplation, see William H. Shannon, *Thomas Merton's Dark Path*, rev. ed. (New York: Farrar, Straus & Giroux, 1987).

God loves people, not practices. I am reminded that Ruth Burrows wrote, "We confuse the means with the end, seeing observances as if they had an absolute value in themselves,"[19] and of the thrust of Merton's last talk on monasticism printed in an appendix of *The Asian Journal of Thomas Merton*. Merton insists that the life of prayer and contemplation not only issue forth in practical action on behalf of the kingdom of God but *are* action on behalf of those others whom God also utters and whose Son died to save. The distinction between prayer and action is a false one because prayer, and a life of prayer, *is* action.

In his introduction to *The Prison Meditations of Fr. Alfred Delp* Merton wrote that to hear our own inner voice (our True Self) is "not simply the decision to accept one's personal salvation from the hands of God, in suffering and tribulation, but the decision to become *totally engaged in the historical task of the Mystical Body of Christ* for the redemption of man and his world" (italics in original).[20] "Our true self," Merton writes in *New Seeds of Contemplation*, is "the self that receives freely and gladly the missions that are God's supreme gifts."[21] I confess that I have had some trouble seeing how some of the "missions" I've been given are

19. Burrows, *Guidelines for Mystical Prayer*, 64.
20. Introduction to Alfred Delp, *The Prison Meditations of Father Alfred Delp* (New York: Herder & Herder, 1963), xxv.
21. Merton, *New Seeds*, 42.

God's *gifts*, but my myopia doesn't change that reality. For Merton, the True Self is a profoundly important connection between the life of prayer and the external world. He writes in the introduction to Delp's meditations, "In finding [God] we find our true selves. We return to the true order [God] has willed for us."[22]

As his monastic life unfolded and matured, Merton learned that we are unlikely to find or, more accurately, be found by God if we isolate ourselves from the rest of humanity in a pink, spiritual haze. He wrote, "God speaks, and God is to be heard, not only on Sinai, not only in my own heart, but in the voice of the stranger." "We must find [God] in our enemy, or we may lose him even in our friend."[23] God speaks in the heart of the stranger because God utters him too. We must listen for God in the enemy because "a partial thought of God" resides there. At every point in human history this has been a very big, and frequently not completed, assignment.

Summary

Whatever Merton said about monastic spirituality is rooted in his convictions that, having discovered the True Self (and thus God within), one must live from

22. Introduction to *Prison Meditations*, xxv.
23. *The Complete Poems of Thomas Merton* (New York: New Directions, 1977), 384.

the inside out, and this interior process of discovery and life of prayer is profoundly related to the world and to engagement with and for it. From a very dislocated youth, Merton began his monastic life, as do many young monastics, filled with a sense of his own "specialness" and the ego-driven quest for God, as if God were something "out there" to be obtained. And, as do monastics who survive and thrive in the life, he changed, he softened, he understood himself to be related to, not separated from, others.

If you read Merton looking for consistency, you are likely to be very disappointed, perhaps even disoriented. Many who have studied Merton's life and particularly his attitudes toward monastic life and his own monastery have noted how widely those attitudes fluctuated. Dom Michael Casey reminds us: "We have the advantage of reading his letters and diaries in sequence with his published work; this gives us some idea of just how much his thought fluctuated. . . . This also suggests that a single quotation need not represent the complexity (or even compatibility) of his views."[24] Exactly so.

In a journal entry on December 10, 1949, Merton recorded a quotation from the poet Rilke that seems applicable to him, as well: "I am the impression that

---

24. Michael Casey, "Thomas Merton and Monastic Renewal," *Cistercian Studies Quarterly* 53, no. 2 (2018): 161.

will change."[25] In a journal entry on January 25, 1964, he mused about "[t]he need for constant self-revision, growth, leaving behind, renunciation of yesterday." The entry continues, "My ideas are always changing, always moving around one center, always seeing the center from somewhere else. I will always be accused of inconsistencies."[26] Merton's "one center" was his monastic commitment. What remained the same for him was the spiritual reality of monastic life; it was the rule, the "trellis" (*regula*), on which he grew. Otherwise he changed. "A man is a free being," he wrote, "who is always changing into himself."[27] "Changing into ourselves" is constantly manifesting the True Self. Merton's life suggests that to mature may not be to become consistent (congruent, yes; consistent, maybe not) so much as to learn what to leave behind.

This chapter has been dense (perhaps in more ways than one!) and has raised several important issues, but perhaps the most important is the question it raises:

25. *Entering the Silence*, The Journals of Thomas Merton, vol. 2: *1941–1952*, ed. Jonathan Montaldo (San Francisco: HarperSanFrancisco, 1996), 377. I am grateful to Dr. Paul Pearson, director of the Thomas Merton Studies Center at Bellarmine University, for locating the quotation for me.

26. *Dancing in the Water of Life*, The Journals of Thomas Merton, vol. 5: *1963–1965*, ed. Robert E. Daggy (San Francisco: HarperSanFrancisco, 1997), 67.

27. Merton, *No Man Is an Island*, 166.

What must you leave behind? Because the less stuff, especially moldy, old, emotional stuff, you drag around, not only will the journey itself be easier, but it will be easier to hear the voice of God within, know the True Self, and by means of it benevolently engage the world. Merton the young monk wrote at the end of his autobiography, "No matter who you are or what you are, you are called to the summit of perfection: you are called to a deep interior life perhaps even to mystical prayer, and to pass the fruits of your contemplation on to others. And if you cannot do so by word, then by example."[28]

28. Thomas Merton, *The Seven Storey Mountain* (New York: Doubleday/Image, 1970), 507.

Chapter 4

Monastic Life: Fleeing the World?

Both *The Seven Storey Mountain* and Merton's early journals[1] record his responses to the serious volunteer work he did in Harlem with Baroness Catherine de Hueck. His poem "Aubade—Harlem," published in *A Man in the Divided Sea* (1946) and dedicated to Baroness de Hueck, speaks of "The ragged dresses of the little children," "the sterile jungles of the waterpipes and ladders," and how Jesus is crucified in Harlem: "Four flowers of blood have nailed Him to the walls of Harlem."[2] Merton's exposure to these realities of economic, racial, and social injustice somehow makes it unsurprising that, after his revelatory Fourth and

---

1. See *Run to the Mountain*, The Journals of Thomas Merton, vol. 1: *1939–1941*, ed. Patrick Hart (San Francisco: HarperSanFrancisco, 1995).

2. *The Collected Poems of Thomas Merton* (New York: New Directions, 1977), 82.

Walnut experience on March 18, 1958, he entered into the Civil Rights struggle, anti–Vietnam War work, opposition to atomic weaponry, and, as Sr. Monica Weis's recent work has shown, ecology.[3]

In late 1960s Merton engaged in a correspondence with feminist theologian Rosemary Radford Ruether. Their exchange of letters published in *At Home in the World*[4] reveals that Ruether's basic message to Merton was along the lines of "if you care so much about the world, leave that Medieval monastery, and get to work out here with us." (The paraphrase is mine.) In mid-March 1967 she wrote to him, "[W]e do not bring paradise out of the wilderness by taking off to the hills, but by struggling with the principalities and powers where they really are."[5] Monastic, contemplative life has always been something of a conundrum to many outside it. Apparently Professor Reuther did not at that point share Merton's presupposition that the "work of prayer" and the life of the monastery *are* an engage-

3. Monica Weis, *The Environmental Vision of Thomas Merton* (Lexington: The University Press of Kentucky, 2011), and "Finding Oneself in the Cosmic Dance: Nature's Grace for Thomas Merton," *Cistercian Studies Quarterly* 50, no. 1 (2015): 65–81.

4. Mary Tardiff, ed., *At Home in the World: The Letters of Thomas Merton and Rosemary Radford Ruether* (Maryknoll, NY: Orbis Books, 1995).

5. Tardiff, *At Home*, 41.

ment with "the principalities and powers." I suspect hers is the common view in society, especially among many Protestants. I hope this chapter might alter it, if only a little.

Shift to chapter 1 of the Gospel of St. Mark. After a brief bit on John the Baptist (1:2-8) and a briefer bit on Jesus' baptism and wilderness temptation (1:9-13), in 1:14-39, Mark describes a "typical day" of Jesus: calling disciples, teaching, healing, and prayer. "In the morning," Mark writes, "while it was still very dark, [Jesus] got up and went out to a deserted place, and there he prayed. And Simon and his companions hunted for him. When they found him they said to him, 'Everyone is searching for you'" (1:35-36). The Greek word for "searching" means " tracking down, hunting with intent to kill." When our Lord withdrew for prayer, his new disciples wanted him to quit wasting time in prayer and get back to the active work of healing and teaching. If not " 'tis ever" at least " 'tis often" thus.

Perhaps we can forgive the disciples since they had been with Jesus only a little while, but their attitude reflects a certain ignorance about the spiritual life. It ignores that, in the words of Evelyn Underhill, human beings "live an amphibious life."[6] Underhill believes that "the meaning of our life is bound up with the

6. Evelyn Underhill, *The Spiritual Life* (Harrisburg, PA: Morehouse Publishing, 1937/1955), 32.

meaning of the universe."[7] We live lives of matter and of spirit; we live in both the visible and tangible world and in the invisible, immaterial world. We say in the Nicene Creed, "I believe in one God, the Father almighty, maker of heaven and earth, of all things *visible and invisible*" (italics mine). This means that there *is* more than is seen, more that is dreamed of in Horatio's philosophy. Activity in one realm affects that in the other. Merton wrote that the unseen world affects the soul. Whether we are conscious of it or not, we Christians *do* behave as if activity in the material world has effects in the spiritual world (and vice versa) or we wouldn't pray prayers of intercession.

All this is background to what Merton says about contemplative and active life, which, in the final analysis, he finds not opposites but *one* life. Most of the essays collected in *Contemplation in a World of Action* speak to this dichotomy in one way or another.[8] Merton addresses the issue head on in an essay in part 1, chapter 8: "Is the World a Problem?," which opens with his parody of himself as "a sort of stereotype of the world-denying contemplative—the man who spurned New York, spat on Chicago, and tromped on Louisville, heading for the woods with Thoreau in one pocket, John of the

7. Underhill, *The Spiritual Life*, 19.

8. Thomas Merton, *Contemplation in a World of Action* (Garden City, NY: Doubleday/Image, 1973).

Cross in another, and holding the Bible open at the Apocalypse."[9]

That essay, and the whole collection, are well worth reading, but in this context I want to highlight the introductory essay in another work, *The Wisdom of the Desert*, which is less well known and both addresses the *fuga mundi* (flight from the world) issue and is one of Merton's best essays (perhaps my favorite). The book is Merton's selection of sayings from the desert Christians of the fourth century, that wonderfully quirky collection of men and women who were among the first Christian monastics, men and women who *did* flee to a literal desert. Merton's essay traces the origins of monastic life and makes connections among the True (or authentic) Self, the life of prayer, and the problems of the world, and there were plenty of those in the fourth century as the Roman Empire crumbled.

For Merton, effective action in the world begins with the quest for the True Self. (See chapter 3.) To put it crudely, if you are really screwed up, you are unlikely to be able to straighten out other people or situations. In a last talk on monasticism Merton made reference to the twelfth-century abbot Adam of Perseigne, who suggested people "come to the monastery, first, to be cured. The period of monastic formation is a period

---

9. Merton, *Contemplation in a World of Action*, 159.

of cure, of convalescence."[10] He noted that the desert monastics *had* to reject the false, formal self, fabricated under social compulsion in "the world." The desert Christian chooses "to lose himself in the inner, hidden reality of a self that was transcendent, mysterious, half-known, and lost in Christ. He had to die to the values of transient existence as Christ had died to them on the cross, and rise from the dead with Him in the light of an entirely new wisdom."[11] Choosing the True Self and desert prayer is allowing oneself to *be* resurrected (note use of the passive voice—resurrection is "done to" one, one must surrender to it), is a resurrective process. The more "resurrected" people there are, the better off the world will be.

But to go to the wilderness (understood as both metaphor and, in some cases, reality), to pray, is not to flee from the evil world; doing that carries the world with one as a standard of comparison. Those desert Christians went to the desert

> to be themselves, their *ordinary* selves. There can
> be no other valid reason for . . . leaving the world.
> And thus to leave the world is . . . to help save

10. *The Asian Journal of Thomas Merton*, ed. N. Burton, P. Hart, and J. Laughlin (New York: New Directions, 1973), 333.

11. Thomas Merton, *The Wisdom of the Desert: Sayings from the Desert Fathers of the Fourth Century* (New York: New Directions, 1960), 7.

it in saving oneself. . . . The Coptic hermits who left the world as though escaping from a wreck, did not merely intend to save themselves. They knew that they were helpless to do any good for others as long as they floundered about in the wreckage. But once they got a foothold on solid ground, things were different. Then they had not only the power but even the obligation to pull the whole world to safety after them.[12]

Because our True Self, the self "spoken as a partial thought of God,"[13] is a reflection of God, it is healing to ourselves and potentially to others. To paraphrase a well-known saying with a monastic, spiritual twist: "physician heal thyself, and thou shalt heal the world."

In the epilogue of his *Basic Principles of Monastic Spirituality*, subtitled "The Monk *in* a Changing World" (italics mine), Merton wrote, "It would be an illusion to think that the monks could live entirely unrelated to the rest of the world."[14] He continued, "[T]hough the monk is withdrawn from the world, he preserves an intimate spiritual contact with those with whom he is actually or potentially united 'in Christ'—the Mystery of our

12. Merton, *Wisdom of the Desert*, 23.

13. "God utters me like a word containing a partial thought of Himself." Merton, *New Seeds of Contemplation* (New York: New Directions, 1961), 37.

14. Thomas Merton, *Basic Principles of Monastic Spirituality* (Springfield, IL: Templegate, 1957/1996), 104.

unity in the Risen Savior, the Son of God."[15] Writing of the prophetic dimension of monasticism in Merton's thought, Ephrem Arcement, OSB, notes Merton understood that "solitude leads to discovery, which leads to healing personal and communal ills, which leads . . . to making way for the kingdom of God to pass through us into our world."[16] Our openness to God heals us, and through that openness God heals the world.

Interestingly, Merton wrote of monks in *Contemplative Prayer* that through prayer "we plunge . . . deep into the heart of that world of which we remain a part although we seem to have 'left' it. In reality we abandon the world only in order to listen more intently to the deepest and most neglected voices that proceed from its inner depths."[17] Merton's later writing speaks of the monk as "marginal person."[18] Being marginal, being "outside the camp" to use biblical language, is crucial *to* the camp one is outside. Just as the person on the sidelines or in the stands can see the game more clearly than those who are playing it, the marginal per-

---

15. Merton, *Basic Principles*, 105.

16. Ephrem Arcement, "Thomas Merton, Saint Bernard, and the Prophetic Dimension of Monasticism in the Early Twenty-First Century," *Cistercian Studies Quarterly* 51, no. 4 (2016): 450.

17. Thomas Merton, *Contemplative Prayer* (Garden City, NY: Doubleday/Image, 1969/1971), 23.

18. See appendix 3 of Merton, *The Asian Journal*.

son, the person who is seeking an authentic self, who has distanced herself from the helter-skelter of modern life, has a much better chance of really *seeing* that life clearly—both its grit and its glory. Merton taught that the world *needs* people who, for Christ's sake, are skeptical about its "givens." "The monk is essentially someone who takes up a critical attitude toward the world and its structures." Merton continues, "[T]he monk is somebody who says, in one way or another, that the claims of the world are fraudulent."[19] As Merton wrote to Jean Leclercq, "The vocation of the monk in the modern world is not survival but prophecy."[20] The role of the marginal person and monk is prophetic.

The vital connection between the mysterious, inner journey of identity and the outer, active journey of response and service is *us*, human beings, individual persons who are willing to love the very society/world we simultaneously refuse by seeing precisely *in* it reflections of Divinity. Merton wrote in *Conjectures of a Guilty Bystander*, "We must contain all divided worlds in ourselves and transcend them in Christ. From that secret . . . unity in myself can . . . come a visible and manifest unity."[21] As we have frequently noted, God

---

19. Merton, *The Asian Journal*, 329.

20. Quoted in Arcement, "Thomas Merton," 454.

21. Thomas Merton, *Conjectures of a Guilty Bystander* (Garden City, NY: Doubleday/Image, 1968), 21.

uttered *everyone* as a "partial thought" of divinity. The task is to see everyone as such.

The prayerful vocation is a profound entry into the world because it is a vocation of identification, the recognition of sameness. This was the focal realization of Merton's Fourth and Walnut experience. Everything comes from a common origin. All is spoken by God. In the biblical book of Genesis God speaks and things come into being. When we deeply understand this, live into it, pray from it, we become God's instruments in the world. When we transcend the divisions in ourselves, we become "unifiers" and "peacemakers" for and with others. In *Thoughts in Solitude* Merton wrote of the mystery of our vocation:

> [T]he love of my man's heart can become God's love for God and men, and my human tears can fall from my eyes as the tears of God because they well up from the motion of His spirit in the heart of His incarnate Son. . . .
>
> When this is learned, then our love of [others] becomes pure and strong. We can go out to them without vanity and without complacency, loving them with something of the purity and gentleness and hiddenness of God's love for us.[22]

22. Thomas Merton, *Thoughts in Solitude* (New York: Farrar, Straus & Giroux/Noonday, 1956/1977), 123–24.

The call is to love others as God loves us, which requires some existential comprehension of God's love for each of us personally. The message of God's love is, or should be, one of the primary proclamations of the Church.

In the sayings of the Desert Christians Merton noted "a repeated insistence on the primacy of love over every-thing else in the spiritual life."[23] He continues, "Love means an interior and spiritual identification with one's brother, so that he is not regarded as an 'object' to 'which' one 'does good.'" As we know, this is the great danger of social service and some forms of social jus-tice work: to "do unto" objects, not persons; to "do unto" rather than to "be with." Merton explains, "Love takes one's neighbour as one's other self. . . . Love demands a complete inner transformation. . . . We have to become, in some sense, the person we love. And this involves a kind of death of our own being, our own self."[24] Attempting to do this involves us in an ultimate, self-emptying (kenotic) Christ-likeness.

The call is to realize that what the prophet Nathan said to King David is true of all of us: "You are the man" or "I am the woman" (2 Sam 12:7). The first step is to recognize my own sinfulness, shortcomings, and shortsightedness. First of all, I'm the problem, not somebody else. Helping novices come gently to

23. Merton, *Wisdom of the Desert*, 17.
24. Merton, *Wisdom of the Desert*, 18.

this realization is an important part of initial monastic formation. Whether or not we are monastics, concern for and action in the world begins within us, with our identification with those whom we wish to serve or with institutions/structures/systems we wish to change. It assumes that *we* have changed, or are in the process of transformation, or, more precisely, submit to *being* transformed. It assumes a coinherence of the material and spiritual worlds, an assumption that action in one influences the other. Some of us make our contribution by prayer and others of us by more active, visible means. Both are important and constructive.

If even in light of these many citations from Merton you think I'm overspiritualizing this relationship, let me say I agree with Desert Father Abbot Pastor: "If you have a chest full of clothing, and leave it for a long time, the clothing will rot inside it. It is the same with the thoughts in our heart. If we do not carry them out by physical action, after a long while they will spoil and turn bad."[25] Furthermore St. Benedict wrote in the Prologue of the Rule of the importance of doing what we know, of what might be termed "good deeds." "[T]he Lord waits for us daily to translate into action . . . his holy teachings."[26]

25. Merton, *Wisdom of the Desert*, 42.
26. Timothy Fry, ed., *The Rule of St. Benedict* (Collegeville, MN: Liturgical Press, 1981), 163.

Here is a final caveat in the matter of how monastic life is related to the needs of the world: There is a great danger in worrying overmuch about success of our prayer and action. In February 1966 Merton wrote a very important letter to Jim Forest, founder of the Catholic Peace Fellowship (and a Merton biographer who has written and spoken widely on Merton[27]): "Do not depend on the hope of results. When you are doing the sort of work you have taken on . . . you may have to face the fact that your work will be apparently worthless and even achieve no result at all."[28] In drawing the letter to a close Merton got to the spiritual heart of the matter, writing, "The real hope . . . is not in something we think we can do, but in God who is making something good out of it in some way we cannot see."[29]

We began this chapter with the close of Jesus' "typical day" and the attempt of his disciples to draw him away from prayer, and we'll close with Jesus. A scribe asked him which commandment was the greatest. Jesus replied, "[Y]ou shall love the Lord your God with all your heart, and with all your soul, and with all your mind, and

27. See, for example, Jim Forest, *Living With Wisdom: A Life of Thomas Merton* (Maryknoll, NY: Orbis Books, 1991).

28. William H. Shannon, ed., *The Hidden Ground of Love: Letters of Thomas Merton on Religious Experience and Social Concerns* (New York: Farrar, Straus & Giroux, 1985), 294.

29. Shannon, ed., *The Hidden Ground*, 297.

with all your strength." He continued, "You shall love your neighbor as yourself" (Mark 12:30-31). In his last talk, "Marxism and Monastic Perspectives," on December 10, 1968, Merton suggested, "The whole purpose of monastic life is to teach men to live by love."[30] By this Merton meant "the translation of *cupiditas* into *caritas*, of self-centered love into an outgoing, other-centered love."[31]

The relationship of prayer and action in monastic life and in the lives of all Christians is rooted in how we love and become conduits of God's love, our having first *been* loved, having accepted that love, and then becoming conduits of it to others, to "the world."[32] In light of all this, perhaps the question is not "What Would Jesus Do," but "Whom would Jesus NOT love?" and then to act accordingly. Nobody's wall sets the limit for our loving.

30. Merton, *The Asian Journal*, 333.
31. Merton, *The Asian Journal*, 334.
32. See 1 John 4:19. All of 1 John 4 is relevant to this matter.

Chapter 5

Obedience and Silence

This chapter begins with two gentle caveats, by way of quotations from Merton. In his late 1960s essay "The Monastic Renewal: Problems and Prospects," Merton stated, "In order to understand monasticism, it is important to concentrate on the *charism of the monastic vocation* rather than on the *structure of monastic institutions or the patterns of monastic observance*" (italics in original).[1] In "Marxism and Monastic Perspectives," Merton's last talk given in Bangkok in 1968, he tells the story of a Tibetan lama who, when faced with the advance of the communists, asked a nearby abbot what his monastery should do. "The abbot," Merton related, "sent back a strange message, which I think is very significant: 'From now on, Brother, everybody

---

1. I quote the essay from *Thomas Merton: Selected Essays*, ed. Patrick F. O'Connell (Maryknoll, NY: Orbis Books, 2013), 391.

stands on his own feet.'" Merton continued, "[W]e can no longer rely on being supported by structures that may be destroyed at any moment. . . . The time for relying on structures has disappeared."[2] Following Merton's distinction, in what follows, we shall be exploring charism, not the structures within which one might exercise it. That being the case, I have chosen to rely not so much on Merton's several essays on monastic renewal, but on what he says about these matters in other contexts.[3]

As we know, the "O word," obedience, isn't very popular. Modern parenting isn't strong on it, at least not as strong as the parents of my childhood were. As a result, modern children sometimes don't learn impulse control over little things and when the big ones of adolescence kick in they are in trouble. The vow of obedience is now regularly omitted from wedding services in some quarters. But forms of the word "obedience" occur three times at the outset of the Rule of St. Benedict: "The labor of obedience [*oboedientiae*] will bring you back to him from whom you had drifted through the sloth of disobedience [*inoboedientiae*]." "This message of mine is for you . . . if you are ready

2. *The Asian Journal of Thomas Merton*, ed. N. Burton, P. Hart, and J. Laughlin (New York: New Directions, 1973), 334.

3. Part 1 of Merton's *Contemplation in a World of Action* (Garden City, NY: Doubleday/Image, 1973) is devoted to monastic renewal.

to give up your own will . . . and armed with the strong and noble weapons of obedience [*oboedientiae*] to do battle for the true King, Christ the Lord."[4]

As well as being a vow in many monastic orders, obedience may be monasticism's ur-virtue and its most misunderstood attitude and practice. It is not about subjugation, domination, and power games.[5] "Humility is a virtue," Merton wrote, "not a neurosis."[6] Monastic obedience is rooted in that of Jesus to the Father and is related to the humility with which Jesus describes himself ("I am gentle and humble of heart"; Matt 11:29) and with which St. Paul characterizes him in Philippians 2:7-8 (which we'll consider shortly). Monastic and Christian humility is about conforming to the image of Christ and developing mastery over the persistent little demon of ego that can manifest as self-assertion, often over things that don't even matter much. "Give me humility," Merton prays in *New Seeds of Contemplation*, "in which alone is rest, and deliver me from pride which

4. Timothy Fry, *The Rule of St. Benedict* (Collegeville, MN: Liturgical Press, 1981), 157.

5. Michael Casey's important essay "Thomas Merton and Monastic Renewal" (*Cistercian Studies Quarterly* 53, no. 2 [2018]: 159–87) devotes significant and insightful attention to obedience.

6. Thomas Merton, *Thoughts in Solitude* (New York: Farrar, Straus & Giroux/Noonday, 1956/1977), 65.

is the heaviest of burdens."[7] Obedience can make us more like Christ and develop in us his love. According to Merton in his essay "The Place of Obedience," it "is a means to closer union with God" and "the chief way by which the monk returns to God."[8] He continued, "Religious obedience must be seen first of all in [the] context of love and discipleship."[9]

We will understand obedience in its monastic context and in Merton's thought better if we know something of the biblical roots of the concept and its etymology. I shall sketch both briefly before returning to Merton's ideas and then, in light of both, shall close this chapter with the peculiar relationship between obedience and silence.

Biblical Roots of Obedience

The roots of monastic obedience are profoundly biblical. God set limits for Adam and Eve in paradise expecting them to obey *for their own good*. They were disobedient. God's greatest gift to Israel was the Torah, which God expected Israel to obey *for the good of their life together*. The basic message of the prophets was

7. Thomas Merton, *New Seeds of Contemplation* (New York: New Directions, 1962), 45.

8. Merton, *Contemplation in a World of Action*, 136.

9. Merton, *Contemplation in a World of Action*, 137.

"return to obedience." The gospel writers depict the obedience of Jesus, none more so than St. John who says Jesus came to do the will of God (John 5:30), to be obedient to God. So Merton says, "Monastic obedience is seen by the monk as a way to imitate the obedience and love of Christ his Master."[10] Indeed, Brendan Freeman, OCSO, in his essay "Interior Silence and Formation," equates "formation of the heart" with "putting on the mind of Christ."[11]

The earliest example of biblical Christology is what many New Testament scholars call the "Christ Hymn" in Philippians 2:6-11.[12] Many think it was an existing hymn that Paul quoted. If so, Christology began not as dogma but as music/singing. Paul introduces the hymn with "Have this mind [the Greek word means something like "habitual disposition"] among yourselves [it's asked of a community] which is yours in Christ Jesus." The habitual disposition of Jesus, the hymn asserts, is that he "came down." "And being found in human form he humbled himself and became obedient to the point of death" (Phil 2:8). Merton alluded to this

10. Merton, *Contemplation in a World of Action*, 136.

11. Brendan Freeman, "Interior Silence and Formation," *Cistercian Studies Quarterly* 49, no. 3 (2014): 400.

12. For more on the Christ hymn, see Bonnie B. Thurston and Judith M. Ryan, *Philippians and Philemon*, Sacra Pagina (Collegeville, MN: Liturgical Press, 2005), 77–92.

text in closing a conference on prayer given to religious women in Calcutta on October 27, 1968: "Our prayer, our surrender to God, is a uniting of ourselves with that obedience whereby He totally surrendered to His Heavenly Father, emptied Himself, obedient unto death."[13] We previously noted that Jesus said, "I am gentle and humble of heart." These two great characteristics of Jesus, humility and obedience, in his world were slave virtues, not held in high regard. Slaves were obedient. Soldiers were obedient. Children were obedient.

Please bear with a little etymology. It will illuminate the relationship between obedience and listening. The Greek word for "obedient" in Luke 2:51 in which Jesus is described as being obedient to his parents (*hupotasso*) is a compound verb made up of "under" and "appoint, designate, order, direct." The form in Luke indicates one under the authority of a superior. The Greek of "became obedient" in the Christ hymn in Philippians 2:8 is also a compound word made up of a preposition and a verb. The preposition *hupo* indicates something under or below.[14] The verb *akouo* means "to hear."

13. Thomas Merton, "Two Conferences on Prayer: India 1968," *The Merton Annual* 31 (2018): 29.

14. In Barclay M. Newman Jr., ed., *A Concise Greek-English Dictionary of the New Testament* (London: United Bible Societies, 1971), *hupo* is translated as "under," "below," and, significantly in this context, "under the authority of" (188).

To be obedient is literally to "hear under," to listen to someone or something who has authority.

Remember that Benedict's Rule opens with the command "Listen!" then thrice uses the word "obedience," which means "listen under." The etymological root of "obedience" in both Greek and Latin (*ob–audire*) is, in fact, a verb for hearing. Obedience has to do with what and to whom we listen because the biblical assumption was that we obey what we hear. In Hebrew "to hear" and "to obey" have the same root. We know someone has heard if he obeys *what* was heard. I recall my mother's sometimes exasperated question "Did you *hear* me?" Translation: Get busy and *do* what I said.

Merton on Obedience

As we turn to what Merton said about obedience, it's important to recall that it was not a theoretical matter for him. I once heard a talk in which "monk" was defined as "a person who wants to live under an abbot." If that is so, a lot depends on the abbot because monastic life assumes obedience to that person. Those who have read Merton's journals or a good biography of him will remember that he struggled with Dom James Fox from whom he was temperamentally very different. This complex relationship is the subject of a fascinating book by Roger Lipsey, *Make Peace Before the Sun Goes Down*, subtitled *The Long Encounter of Thomas Merton and His*

Abbot, James Fox.[15] Michael Casey describes monastic obedience as "a deliberate and heartfelt abandonment of self-will as an act of personal discipleship."[16] This makes obedience to an abbot with whom one has difficulties not only more challenging but a matter of spiritual importance of the first order. It was my privilege to know Dom Flavian Burns, Merton's last abbot, who told me Dom Fox once said he had no more obedient monk than Fr. Louis, Thomas Merton.

In an essay called "The Place of Obedience" Merton notes, "The obedience of the monk must therefore be the obedience of faith, deeply rooted in his belief in Christ as his Lord and Savior, in his earnest desire to live as a perfect disciple of Christ . . . who for our sakes became 'obedient unto death'" He continues, "Monastic obedience is seen by the monk as a way to imitate the obedience of Christ his Master. Since Jesus 'emptied himself taking the form of a servant' . . . the monk will seek also to empty himself of his own will and to become a servant, above all because this is Christ's 'new commandment.'"[17] (One recalls in this context that Jesus said, "a disciple is not above his master" [Matt 10:24]). Merton goes on: "Religious obedience

15. Roger Lipsey, *Make Peace Before the Sun Goes Down* (Boston & London: Shambala, 2015).

16. Casey, "Thomas Merton and Monastic Renewal," 174.

17. Merton, *Contemplation in a World of Action*, 136.

must be seen first of all in this context of love and discipleship." And: "The whole purpose of monastic obedience . . . is the sanctification of the monk and in fact his liberation from temporal agitations and concerns in order that he may learn to listen to God in his heart and to obey God."[18]

Years before that essay Merton had written in *No Man Is an Island,* "Obedience to man has no meaning unless it is primarily obedience to God."[19] When we get to the chapters on prayer it will be useful to remember that, at the very end of his life, he also said, "Christian obedience is much, much deeper than just the problem of authority. . . . Prayer itself is obedience. Our deepest obedience takes place when we pray. Prayer is an act of surrender; it is essentially an act of surrender to God's love."[20] This has enormous implications for the practice and premises of prayer.

The obedience Benedict's Rule envisions is the obedience of Jesus to God. It is probably only possible in situations where everyone has the good of the *other* at heart. The monk can be obedient because, as Merton says, "the superior first of all must see that he is obliged to serve and preserve the spiritual liberty of his

18. Merton, *Contemplation in a World of Action*, 137 and 138.
19. Thomas Merton, *No Man Is an Island* (New York: Doubleday/Image, 1955/1967), 35.
20. Merton, "Two Conferences on Prayer," 28.

subjects."[21] Obedience re-forms in Christ the one who is obedient when the one to whom he/she is obedient has his/her best interests at heart. This, for example, is why mutual obedience is appropriate in Christian marriage: each has the other's best interest at heart. Thus the Ephesian letter can command "*Be subject to one another* out of reverence for Christ" (Eph 5:21, italics mine).

The monastic context of obedience is the common quest for God, the shared desire to be more Christ-like and thus concern to serve others as Christ has served us. "Obedience," Merton writes, "then becomes an expression of the new life and the new creation which restores the simplicity and peace of paradise (*paradises claustralis*) to communal life in which each is the servant of all, and each finds fulfillment in a meaningful service of love . . . vivified by the presence of Christ in his Spirit."[22]

Obedience and Silence

As I have considered what Merton suggests about obedience, it has occurred to me that the virtue of obedience and the practice of silence go hand in hand. By its etymology, "obedience" has to do with what and to

21. Merton, *No Man Is an Island*, 140.
22. Merton, *No Man Is an Island*, 140.

whom we "listen under." I had long since drafted this chapter when a Lenten reflection by Fr. Richard Gula, PSS, appeared in *Give Us This Day*. Fr. Gula confirmed my intuition: "Obedience to God requires discernment. Listening is key. Attention must be paid." Listen, he says, because "the murmurings of the heart may be messages from God."[23]

Sara Maitland's *A Book of Silence,* a memoir of living in a hermitage in Galloway, Scotland, brought the importance of silence to the attention of many in the United Kingdom (where she writes for *The Tablet*) and the United States (where she has appeared several times in *The Christian Century*).[24] The theme has appeared in the secular press in Susan Cain's book on introverts titled *Quiet*[25] and in two books in 2018 that the reviewer in *The Economist* described as attempting "to pursue silence with nets of word."[26] Apparently what St. Benedict and his children have always known is being rediscovered in more secular contexts.

23. Richard Gula, "Genuinely Alive," *Give Us This Day* 9, no. 3 (March 2019): 83.

24. Sara Maitland, *A Book of Silence* (London: Granta, 2008).

25. Susan Cain, *Quiet* (New York: Broadway Paperbacks, 2013).

26. Reviews of Alain Corbin, *A History of Silence*, trans. Jan Birrell (Cambridge: Polity, 2018), and Erling Kagge, *Silence: In the Age of Noise*, trans. Becky Crook (London: Pantheon, 2018), in *The Economist*, "Where of We Cannot Speak," May 19, 2018, page 78.

Nobody hears very well or can listen attentively in a noisy, static-filled environment. The subtle, gentle messages of the Spirit to whom we must be obedient are often obscured by the general racket in which we live and, most tragically now, which we *choose* to generate with our gizmos. I have personally observed a lot of these devices in monastic houses and monastic hands. Merton worried about "chat" long before the advent of the cell phone and tablet computer. He wrote to Dom Aelred Graham in December 1963, ". . . I think it is terribly important to preserve the contemplative dimension of silence, aloneness, and so on. . . . There is much danger of it getting lost in some of our Cistercian monasteries where they are beginning to get very chatty."[27] There are very few places in the world where one can go to be silent. In making reference to an age of totalitarianism, Merton spoke correctly of "the murderous din of our materialism." It is murderous because it drowns out the Word.[28]

As Merton noted in the 1960s, even in some monastic houses, noise has become habitual and almost unnoticed. We in the world wonder why we get tired when an extraordinary amount of our unconscious energy is drained by filtering out the distractions and noise, a fair amount of which is, in reality, under our control. It is an

27. Thomas Merton, *The School of Charity (Letters on Religious Renewal and Spiritual Direction)*, ed. Patrick Hart (New York: Harvest HBJ Book, 1990), 188.

28. Merton, *Thoughts in Solitude*, 12.

uncomfortable truth that many of us have a lot of freedoms we don't choose to exert or exercise. It's easier to drift along or to enjoy complaining about what we don't like than to choose and to act, in this case, to put up with or generate noise rather than to switch off or unplug.

Ubiquitous noise isn't normal. But we are beginning to accept it as such, and all the little demons cheer and wag their forked tails in glee. If we cannot listen, if we cannot hear clearly, we cannot know to what or to whom we should be obedient. And, more fundamentally than that, we cannot know who we are. For a number of people the inability to be quiet and alone is because they are afraid of themselves (perhaps because they still operate out of a False Self), afraid of what they might hear and, therefore, of what they might have to *do* to be obedient in response to what is heard. In *Markings* Dag Hammarskjold wrote of being "able to see, hear, and attend to that within us which *is* there in the darkness and the silence."[29] At about the same time Merton wrote, "My knowledge of myself in silence . . . opens out into the silence . . . of God's own self."[30] Then what?

The monastic virtue of obedience is profoundly connected to the monastic practice of silence, which itself is entwined with solitude, which we shall consider in the

29. Dag Hammarskjold, *Markings* (New York: Alfred A. Knopf, 1964), 97.

30. Merton, *Thoughts in Solitude*, 70. As an earlier chapter in this book indicated, Merton understood that God is resident within us.

next chapter. In a healthy monastery, as in a healthy family, with authentic and appropriate structures, through the labor of obedience, one becomes more Christ-like and thereby returns to God. This is why Benedict called obedience "all-powerful and righteous arms" for our "fight under the true King, the Lord Jesus Christ." The language, especially the military metaphor, may in our day and age make us squirmy and uncomfortable, but the *bonum obedientiae* (which Merton translates the "benefit of obedience"[31]) remains "a means to closer union with God. It is, in fact, the chief way by which the monk returns to God."[32] In his poem "In Silence" Merton presents the challenge.

In Silence

Be still
Listen to the stones of the wall.
Be silent, they try
To speak your

Name.
Listen
To the living walls.
Who are you?
Who
Are you? Whose
Silence are you?

31. Merton, *Contemplation in a World of Action*, 136.
32. Merton, *Contemplation in a World of Action*, 136.

Who (be quiet)
Are you (as these stones
Are quiet). Do not
Think of what you are
Still less of
What you may one day be.
Rather
Be what you are (but who?) be
The unthinkable one
You do not know.

O be still, while
You are still alive,
And all things live around you
Speaking (I do not hear)
To your own being,
Speaking by the Unknown
That is in you and in themselves.

"I will try, like them
To be my own silence:
And this is difficult. The whole
World is secretly on fire. The stones
Burn, even the stones
They burn me. How can a man be still or
Listen to all things burning? How can he dare
To sit with them when
All their silence
Is on fire?"[33]

---

33. *The Collected Poems of Thomas Merton* (New York: New Directions, 1977), 280–81. Used with permission.

All this being so, the real, personal question for both monks and the rest of us is "To whom do I listen?" *Really* listen? How much silence can I create, appropriate, and *be* in order to listen toward God, toward the "partial thought" of God that I am? "Prayer," Merton reminds us in *Thoughts in Solitude*, "is the orientation of our whole body, mind and spirit to God in silence, attention, and adoration." "My life is a listening," he wrote; "[God's] is a speaking. My salvation is to hear and respond. For this, my life must be silent."[34]

34. Merton, *Thoughts in Solitude*, 48 and 74.

Chapter 6

Monastic Solitude

A Biographical Reminder

As we prepare to consider monastic solitude and its possible parallels outside monastic life, I remind you of some aspects of Merton's biography. In December 1941 he entered the Trappist Abbey of Gethsemani and loved the life, but by the early 1950s, he was exploring other monastic options, including the more eremitical Camaldolese Order or becoming a hermit somewhere more remote than near Bardstown, Kentucky. Historically there had been almost no tradition of hermits in the Cistercian Order. Merton continually requested it be considered. At first, his abbot gave him permission to spend time in a shed in Gethsemani's woods, St. Anne's. On February 9, 16, 17, and 18, 1953, Merton wrote movingly in his journal of time spent at St. Anne's and of his desire for greater solitude.[1] Eventually a small,

---

1. *A Search for Solitude*, The Journals of Thomas Merton, vol. 3, *1952–1960*, ed. Lawrence S. Cunningham (San Francisco: Harper-SanFrancisco, 1996), 29–30 and 32–34.

cinderblock building was built on the monastery prop-
erty, and Merton was allowed to spend the day there.
Finally, in 1965 he was given permission to live there
full time as a hermit. As we consider his reflections on
solitude, it is well to bear in mind that within ten years
of monastic profession the hermit life became central
to his vocation.

Merton prefaces *No Man Is an Island* by saying, ". . .
I only desire in this book to share with the reader my own
reflections on certain aspects of the spiritual life."[2] An important aspect of it is Merton's insistence on the critical
place of solitude in monastic life. "The one thing that
most truly makes a monk what he is," Merton writes,
"is this irrevocable break with the world and all that is in
it, in order to seek God in solitude."[3] Spiritual solitude
is prefaced by skepticism about mainstream society and
its goals and givens. If God is to be found in cenobitic
monastic life, a certain amount of solitude is required.

It is important to remember that solitude is not the
same as loneliness (although many solitaries experience loneliness from time to time, as do people who
live in religious communities and families). In a long
article addressing loneliness as a public health problem
that appeared in *The Economist*, loneliness was defined
by researchers as "*perceived* social isolation," whereas

2. Thomas Merton, *No Man Is an Island* (Garden City, NY:
Doubleday/Image, 1955/1976), 7.

3. Merton, *No Man Is an Island*, 116.

solitude "implies a choice to be alone."[4] The study suggested that functionally, the essential difference between the two is volitional. And yet even chosen solitude can be viewed askance by others not so inclined.

In American society, for example, unless you fell in love with Henry David Thoreau in high school English class, solitude is likely to have negative connotations. Solitaries are "losers," unable to attract a spouse or partner, social misfits, friendless, misogynistic. You may even have heard this about monastics in general. In stark contrast, Merton suggests we cannot mature as human beings without some measure of solitude, and, as we noted in the previous chapter, this is because solitude goes hand in hand with the silence necessary for spiritual listening. Merton wrote, "Without solitude of some sort there is and can be no maturity. Unless one becomes empty and alone, he cannot give himself in love because he does not possess the deep self which is the only gift worthy of love."[5]

4. "Alone in the Crowd," *The Economist*, September 1, 2018, 49. The article (pages 49–51) noted that 35 percent of Americans over forty-five were lonely and some studies likened "its impact on health to obesity or smoking 15 cigarettes per day" (49). An article in *AARP Magazine* detailed the health risks of loneliness: Lynn Darling, "Is There a Cure for Loneliness?" (December 2019/January 2020): vol. 63, no. 1B, pp. 50–55.

5. Thomas Merton, "Notes for a Philosophy of Solitude," in *Disputed Questions* (New York: Farrar, Straus & Cudahy, 1960), 206–7. (Hereafter in the text as DQ.)

Many of society's ills that Merton so eloquently diagnosed are rooted in the inability to be alone. As Desert Father Abba Moses told a brother who asked for a good word, "Go, sit in your cell, and your cell will teach you everything."[6] Blaise Pascal (he of the famous "wager") concurred, "All the unhappiness of men arises from one single fact, that they cannot stay quietly in their own chamber."[7] But there seems to be a conspiracy to prevent the sort of solitude that would lead to critical analysis of "the way things are" and "what they say." This being the case, whether "the herd" is in "the world" or in the monastery, we might all perish from a bad case of "herd mentality." Importantly, the solitude Merton advocates is not necessarily geographic or exterior. It may well be internal and spiritual. People living in communities or in families may well develop spiritual solitude or spiritual aloneness. In an important essay on interior silence and monastic formation, Brendan Freeman, OCSO, writes that solitude is "distinguished from isolation, from reclusion and separation," and that it implies "that the outside world was shut out but the inner world was present." Freeman explains, "The soli-

6. Thomas Merton, *The Wisdom of the Desert: Sayings from the Desert Fathers of the Fourth Century* (New York: New Directions, 1960), 30.

7. Blaise Pascal, *Pensées* (New York: Washington Square Press, 1965), 43 (# 139).

tude of the heart . . . is always present."[8] Put another way, one can always withdraw into the cave of the heart, which Hindu thought calls the *guha*. We always carry our own solitude within us and always have access to it.

Most of the rest of this chapter is a summary of Merton's extended reflection on solitude that appears in "Notes for a Philosophy of Solitude," only one of his many works devoted to the subject.[9] The essay's publication history is noteworthy and interesting. In 1955 Merton published an article in a French journal titled "Dans le desert de Dieu." It appeared in expanded form in English in 1960 as "The Solitary Life"[10] and then was expanded as the long essay "Notes for a Philosophy of Solitude" in *Disputed Questions* (1960). (Citations of this essay throughout the rest of the chapter will appear

---

8. Brendan Freeman, "Interior Silence and Formation," *Cistercian Studies Quarterly* 49, no. 3 (2014): 402 and 403.

9. An excellent overview of Merton on solitude is John F. Teahan, "Solitude: A Central Motif in Thomas Merton's Life and Writings," *The Journal of the American Academy of Religion* 50, no. 4 (December 1982): 521–38. Teahan notes, "Merton saw solitude at the heart of the monastic ideal" (523) and also understood that "solitude is never simply a matter of Terrestrial space" (531). See also Douglas Burton-Christie, "The Work of Loneliness: Thomas Merton's Experiments in Solitude," *Anglican Theological Review* 88, no. 1 (Winter 2006): 25–45.

10. It was included in Thomas Merton, *The Monastic Journey*, ed. Patrick Hart (Kalamazoo, MI: Cistercian Publications, 1977), 151–62.

in parentheses in the text; the edition quoted is the one found in *Disputed Questions* ([DQ].) In a letter on March 5, 1968, Merton called the essay "very central" to his work.[11] That being the case I have summarized its three sections: The Tyranny of Division; In the Sea of Perils; Spiritual Poverty. But note at the outset that Merton says the essay might also be called "Philosophy of Monastic Life" since he is "speaking of the solitary spirit which is really essential to the monastic view of life, but which is not confined to monasteries" (DQ 177). Solitude is another aspect of Merton's monastic spirituality that translates to life "outside the walls." It may be as important outside the cloister as within it.

Part 1: The Tyranny of Division

This section of the essay has nine numbered sections. I shall introduce only the first four, which are foundational: (1) renounce diversion, (2) accept our own absurdity, (3) take responsibility for our own inner life, (4) recognize that solitude is not always geographic.

1. Renounce Diversion

In one way or another Merton suggests that we are being entertained to perdition. We are victims of

11. William H. Shannon, ed., *The Hidden Ground of Love: The Letters of Thomas Merton on Religious Experience and Social Concerns* (New York: Farrar, Straus & Giroux, 1985), 642.

"diversion, systematic distraction," what Pascal called *divertissement*: "Diversion amuses us, and leads us unconsciously to death."[12] Its purpose is to "anesthetize the individual as individual . . . in the warm apathetic stupor of . . . collectivity" (DQ 178). People are encouraged, perhaps coerced, to devote themselves to acquisition, status, ego gratification. In a sermon called "Taking Jesus Seriously," Marcus Borg suggested something similar, "that the central values of modern Western culture are centered in what I have called the three *A*s—appearance, affluence, and achievement." "Driven by these values," Borg says, "we become blind to much else."[13] Exactly so. Additionally, Merton warns against "spiritual amusement" (DQ 180), playing at church, being so busy with the forms and externals (even "good works") that we develop no interior life in Christ. This is a great temptation, especially, I think, for many devout laypersons.

2. Accept Our Own Absurdity

Merton says our first task is to accept the absurdity of this situation by renouncing pointless diversions. We have to allow illusions about ourselves to be shattered. Merton writes, "The solitary is one who is critical first

12. Pascal, *Pensées*, 45 (# 171).

13. Marcus J. Borg, *Days of Awe and Wonder* (New York: Harper Collins/Harper One, 2017), 126. The sermon was preached at Calvary Episcopal Church, Memphis, TN, March 17, 1997.

of all of himself" (DQ 194). Solitaries "know the evils that are in other men because they experience these evils first of all in themselves" (DQ 194). (We noted a similar idea in chapter 4.) In short, I must realize that the story I tell myself about me may not be your story of who I am. In this regard Pascal said we should be grateful to those who point out our faults to us.[14] And in the essay quoted above, Brendan Freeman says, "Awareness of our failings and sins is one of the greatest graces we can receive." This is because "it can lead to compunction, conversion and compassion."[15]

3. Take Responsibility for Our Own Inner Lives

Knowing that God lives in us and we in God, we must take responsibility for our own inner lives (DQ 180). Here, again, silence and solitude are closely aligned. We listen for "the unspeakable beating of a Heart within the heart of one's own life" (DQ 180). In *New Seeds of Contemplation* Merton wrote that God "comes down from heaven and finds us. . . . We become contemplatives when God discovers Himself in us."[16] Whether monastic or not, once one recognizes

14. Pascal, *Pensées*, 152 (# 535).

15. Freeman, "Interior Silence," 409.

16. Thomas Merton, *New Seeds of Contemplation* (New York: New Directions, 1961), 39. Freeman suggests that "our hearts are where Jesus is praying continuously to the Father" (401).

this existential truth, the reality of God within, he or she must choose or reject it and live with the consequences of that decision.

4. Recognize That Solitude Is Not Always Geographic

We must realize that solitude may not be geographic. Although it might be, what is called for is not necessarily "flight into the desert" as a physical place so much as individuation of thought and prayer, maintaining always the cave of the heart. Solitude is attitudinal as much as it is actual. It invites one to step outside one's mental box. One sets aside the herd mentality and thinks for herself. One develops "an emptiness of heart." All this may separate one from the mainstream. But monastic spirituality is not geared to make one "mainstream." It is, Merton suggests, "a vocation to become *fully awake*" (DQ 184). As the tortoise carries his home with him, we each carry with us our own essential solitude. And that essential, internal solitude facilitates the clarity of our sight and thus our evaluation of society, its values, ideas, and "givens."

Part 2: In the Sea of Perils

Part 2 of the study is divided into twenty-two numbered sections. Merton begins by asserting that the point of solitude is solidarity; if it is authentic, it leads to a deeper and more authentic unity among people (DQ

186). "The true solitary does not renounce anything that is basic and human about his relationship to [others]" (DQ 186). Merton's call is to renounce "arbitrary social imagery" for a certain emptiness and simplicity. "Arbitrary social imagery" refers to the fictions society feeds us about identity and "the way things are" and so is related to the False Self discussed in chapter 3. The solitary must reject these false images. But "[w]hat the solitary renounces is not his union with [others] . . . but rather the deceptive fictions and inadequate symbols which tend to take the place of genuine social unity." Perhaps paradoxically, the solitary seeks solidarity with others. This is "the doorway by which he enters into the mystery of God and brings others into that mystery by the power of his love and humility" (DQ 188–89). By entering into the mystery of God and living it, we demonstrate its reality to others and thereby invite others to join us in a more authentic spiritual life.

We can't take people places we haven't been. We begin, as did the Desert Christians described in Merton's *The Wisdom of the Desert*, by healing the wounds in ourselves and discovering therein a means to heal the wounds of the world. We must be on our guard, Merton says, "against our natural obsession with the visible, social and communal forms of Christian life, which tend at times to be inordinately active" (DQ 191). The solitary gently refuses the myths and fictions of social life (a subset of which can be the social life of a parish), especially the fiction of "over-doing."[17] For those of us who live outside the monastery, the solitary vocation is to simplicity, silence, poverty, emptiness, anonymity. This withdrawal (or detachment or choice to be marginal) is a special form of love. The solitary "opts out" because she loves the world. When one makes radical room for God by a decision toward interior solitude, one makes room for what God cares most about, and that is usually what the world passes by, considers useless or "throw-away."

Toward the end of part 2, Merton lifts up two important caveats. First, the sort of solitude under consideration requires volition or choice. It is a special "vocation" that must be "elected by a deep interior decision." And it may well involve "bitter suffering." It's not for everybody (DQ 196). Second, solitude as he speaks of it is not flight into a "protesting minority" (DQ 198). Merton recognizes the danger of false consolation in the company of like-minded protestors. Those of us who lived through the 1960s know that groups that define themselves in terms of what they are

17. In my view, a great problem in much of contemporary Protestantism is its obsession with activity (whether that be worship or service projects), especially "good works" without equal attention to the development of the interior life, knowledge of self, and the surrender of its falsities to God's reshaping. Like fish swimming around looking for water, we think maybe by swimming we invent it.

"against" with no clear notion of what they are "for" can become as insular and dangerous as what they protest, perhaps even more so.

Merton says the true solitary "is called to the nakedness and hunger of a more primitive and honest condition. The condition of a stranger (*xeniteia* [the word Merton uses]) and a wanderer on the face of the earth, who has been called out of what was familiar . . . in order to seek strangely and painfully after what he knows not" (DQ 198). It is reminiscent of the call of God to Abram who was seventy-five when God told him to "go," but not where. "In the eyes of conformist society, the hermit is nothing but a failure. . . . [The hermit] is outside all our projects, plans, assemblies, movements" (DQ 199). And this, of course, is the point. "The empty horizons of the solitary life enable us to grow accustomed to a light that is not seen where the mirage of secular pursuits fascinates and deludes our gaze" (DQ 200). This sort of solitary must (at least occasionally) leave the lights of the city to see the stars in the night sky, a particularly apt metaphor for our age.

Part 3: Spiritual Poverty

The final section of Merton's essay addresses being "unproductive." We live in a society that marginalizes the "unproductive," for example, the unborn, the chronically ill, the elderly, the mentally ill, the addicted.

In a culture that values only those who "produce," the solitary may be at best disliked and ignored and at worst profoundly despised and persecuted. Society comes after the solitary as St. Peter came after our Lord who withdrew in prayer and says, "Get busy," not recognizing that prayer, awareness, and aliveness, the solitary's contribution, are a very different sort of "busy" and an important "work."

The monastic solitary and especially the solitary in the world has to make peace with the poverty of not accomplishing much in a visible, much less saleable, way. The canvas on which a solitary paints his life may be an unseen one, but no less beautiful for that, and no less pleasing to God than more active and visible work. Merton says again, "[N]o one should try it [solitude, eremitic life] unless he has some assurance that he really has been called to it by God" (DQ 204). "One cannot rashly presume to become a solitary merely by his own will" (DQ 204). "Indeed there is a special irony about solitude in community: that if you are called to solitude by God, even if you live in a community your solitude will be inescapable" (DQ 205). The "community" in question could be a family or a parish or workplace as well as a monastery.

Clearly Merton understands that solitude is an attitude of heart as much as it is a geographic situation, being alone. He uses the traditional term "recollection" as "almost the same thing as interior solitude. It is in recollection that we discover . . . the infinite solitude of God dwelling within us."[18] Again, the principle of "God within" as the source of the True Self is in evidence. It is an extraordinary perception—spiritual solitude can give one insight into the inner life of God:

> We become solitaries not when we realize how alone we are, but when we sense something of the solitude of God. His solitude . . . makes us all the more truly the brothers of all things.
>
> We cannot live for others until we have entered this solitude.[19]

Conclusion

In closing this summary of some of Merton's thought on solitude, I return to a quotation from the outset of the chapter: "Unless one becomes empty and alone, he cannot give himself in love because he does not possess the deep self which is the only gift worthy of love" (DQ 206–7). In the final analysis, solitude, whether it be internal or geographic, in monastic life or "in the world," if it is genuine and a God-given call, will issue forth in deeper and more inclusive love. One refuses distractions, "listens under" all the exterior racket of life,

18. Merton, *No Man Is an Island*, 171.
19. Merton, *No Man Is an Island*, 171.

enters the cave of the heart, and emerges with clearer sight and more disinterested love. As Merton wrote in the essay "Monastic Renewal: Renewal and Discipline," "[D]iscipline means solitude of some sort, not in the sense of selfish withdrawal but in the sense of an emptiness that no longer cherishes the comfort of various social 'idols' and is not slavishly dependent on the approval of others. In such solitude one learns not to seek love but to *give* it" (italics in original).[20]

Merton's poem, "Song: If You Seek . . . ," summarizes all this beautifully:

> If you seek a heavenly light
> I, Solitude, am your professor!
>
> I go before you into emptiness,
> Raise strange suns for your new mornings,
> Opening the windows
> Of your innermost apartment.
>
> When I, loneliness, give my special signal
> Follow my silence, follow where I beckon!
> Fear not, little beast, little spirit
> (Thou word and animal)
> I, Solitude, am angel
> And have prayed in your name.

20. Thomas Merton, part 1, "Monastic Renewal," section 5, "Renewal and Discipline," in *Contemplation in a World of Action* (Garden City, NY: Doubleday/Image, 1973), 132.

Look at the empty, wealthy night
The pilgrim moon!
I am the appointed hour,
The "now" that cuts
Time like a blade.

I am the unexpected flash
Beyond "yes," beyond "no,"
The forerunner of the Word of God.

Follow my ways and I will lead you
To golden-haired suns,
Logos and music, blameless joys,
Innocent of questions
And beyond answers:

For I, Solitude, am thine own self.
I, Nothingness, am thy All.
I, Silence, am thy Amen![21]

21. *The Collected Poems of Thomas Merton* (New York: New Directions, 1977), 340. Used with permission.

Chapter 7

Merton's Principles of Prayer (Part 1)[1]

Thomas Merton wrote an enormous amount about prayer, by which he usually meant *wordless* prayer. One might even make the case that, in one way or another, *everything* he wrote was about prayer, was directly related to prayer, or arose from prayer. One of the early full-length secondary studies of Merton's writing was *Thomas Merton on Prayer* by John J. Higgins, SJ.[2] Although it began its life as a 1965 article in *Collectanea Cisterciensia* and appeared in various forms in the late

---

1. Some of the material in this chapter appeared previously in my essay "'Rising Up Out of the Center': Thomas Merton on Prayer," *The Merton Annual* 20 (2007): 109–22. Much of this number is devoted to Merton and prayer. I am grateful to the editors for permission to use it here.

2. John J. Higgins, *Thomas Merton on Prayer* (Garden City, NY: Doubleday/Image, 1975).

1960s, Merton's *The Climate of Monastic Prayer* was published in 1969 and reprinted in 2018 as Merton's last book.[3] All this being the case, it is interesting that, to my knowledge, in only one instance did he describe how he himself prayed. It was in response to a question from Pakistani scholar of Sufism Abdul Aziz, in a letter of January 2, 1966, in a correspondence that is one of the most comprehensive records we have of a Muslim-Christian dialogue in the twentieth century.[4]

While it is fascinating to unpack the Islamic concepts to which Merton alludes in the full passage in the letter (which is well worth reading in its entirety), here, in brief, is what Merton says about his own "method of meditation." "I have a very simple way of prayer. It is centered entirely on attention to the presence of God and to His will and His love. . . . One might say this gives my meditation the character . . . [of] 'being before God as if you saw Him.'"[5] Merton continues, "My

3. Thomas Merton, *The Climate of Monastic Prayer* (Collegeville, MN: Liturgical Press, 2018).

4. The Catholic University of America scholar Sidney H. Griffith has written on Merton and Islam and specifically on the Abdul Aziz letters. See his "'As One Spiritual Man to Another': The Merton-Abdul Aziz Correspondence," in *Merton and Sufism: The Untold Story*, ed. Rob Baker and Gray Henry (Louisville, KY: Fons Vitae Press, 1999), 101–29.

5. William H. Shannon, ed., *The Hidden Ground of Love: The Letters of Thomas Merton on Religious Experience and Social Concerns* (New York: Farrar, Straus & Giroux, 1985), 63.

prayer is then a kind of praise rising up out of the center of Nothing and Silence. If I am still present 'myself' this I recognize as an obstacle about which I can do nothing unless [God] removes the obstacle. . . . Such is my ordinary way of prayer, or meditation. It is not 'thinking about' anything but a direct seeking of the Face of the Invisible, which cannot be found unless we become lost in Him who is Invisible."[6]

From Merton's description of his own prayer I suggest the following five principles of prayer, each of which will be considered in more detail in this chapter:

1. God is with us.

2. Prayer is a gift and, as such, can't really be taught.

3. In prayer it is crucial to be present. We start where we are.

4. Two difficulties in prayer are distractions and self-consciousness.

5. Intentionally and potentially all of life is prayer.

1. God Is with Us.

This is a fundamental assertion of Christianity. We call our Lord "Emmanuel," "God with us" (Matt 1:23). Merton describes his prayer as primarily a matter of "attention to the presence of God." In *Spiritual Direction*

6. Shannon, ed., *Hidden Ground*, 64.

and Meditation (1959) he wrote that "the ultimate end of all mental prayer is communion with God"[7] and that "not only in the future *but also here and now*" (italics in original).[8] St. Teresa of Avila is reputed to have said that all difficulties in prayer begin with the assumption that God is somewhere else. Merton would agree. God is not absent but present. If there is a "connectivity problem," it is on the human end of the line (a metaphor for those of you who remember telephone landlines).

In *Spiritual Direction and Meditation* Merton spoke of "*the union that is already truly effected between our souls and God by grace*" (italics in original).[9] God is already present in three senses. (Please excuse the grammar lesson. I started life as an English teacher. One never quite recovers.) God is present in an adjectival, geographic sense: here, at hand, "among us." God is present in an adverbial, temporal sense: now existing. Third, God is present in a nominal sense: as gift voluntarily given. Thus Merton stressed in the letter to Aziz, "*faith* by which alone we can know the presence of God."[10] Prayer, like faith, is a gift, not accomplishment.

7. Thomas Merton, *Spiritual Direction and Meditation* (Collegeville, MN: Liturgical Press, 1960), 61.

8. Merton, *Spiritual Direction and Meditation*, 64.

9. Merton, *Spiritual Direction and Meditation*, 67.

10. Shannon, ed., *Hidden Ground*, 63.

In some mysterious way the one who prays must trust that God is here, present. Of this matter Ruth Burrows wrote in *Guidelines for Mystical Prayer,* "The key word is 'trust.' And trust demands humility." She continued, "We must learn to trust, refusing to set any value on what is felt, whether it be consolation or suffering."[11] An English contemporary of Merton's who wrote on prayer, Olive Wyon, concurred, "All our prayer . . . consists in wanting God. . . . What we *feel* when we are quiet before God does not matter in the least."[12] Prayer is not so much something we *do* as something we receive. From this the next point logically proceeds.

2. Prayer Is a Gift and, as Such, Can't Really Be "Taught."

Prayer is centered on attention to the presence of God known by faith. Prayer is not, Merton writes in *Contemplative Prayer*, "a psychological trick but a theological grace. It can come to us *only* as a gift, and not as the result of our clever use of spiritual techniques."[13]

---

11. Ruth Burrows, *Guidelines for Mystical Prayer* (New York: Paulist Press, 1976/2017), 40 and 43.

12. Olive Wyon, *Prayer* (London: Collins/Fontana, 1962/1966), 118.

13. Thomas Merton, *Contemplative Prayer* (Garden City, NY: Doubleday/Image, 1971), 92.

One remembers at this point Merton's understanding
of the True Self and his insistence that God is resident
within humans who are partial thoughts of God. Perhaps in some instances we might think of prayer as God
speaking to himself within us.

The logical implication of prayer as gift (grace) is
that, actually, prayer can't be taught as a technique
(although techniques or "methods" of prayer can be
helpful). One might assist another person to be dis-
posed toward receiving the gift of prayer, putting oneself where he or she can be found, but a person can't
teach another to pray because prayer is as individuated
as a fingerprint, as DNA. Just as each of us must find
the thought of God's self that God speaks in us, each
of us must find our own way to pray, our own "name
for God" if you will. Writing on June 15, 1964, to
Etta Gullick, who was charged with spiritual formation of Anglican ordinands at St. Stephen's College,
Oxford,[14] Merton said, "I do not think contemplation
can be taught, but certainly an aptitude for it can be

14. Merton had an extended correspondence with Gullick, whom
he called his "sister," in the United Kingdom. His letters to her are
important sources of information about his thoughts on prayer. For
more, see Bonnie Thurston, "'Almost as if I Had a Sister'—Introducing the Merton-Gullick Correspondence," *The Merton Journal*
24, no. 2 (Advent 2017): 16–25, and "Spiritual Formation & 'Progress in Prayer' in the Merton-Gullick Letters," *The Merton Journal*
25, no. 1 (Eastertide 2018): 31–42.

awakened." He continued, "[I]t is a question of show-
ing . . . in a mysterious way by example how to proceed. Not by the example of doing, but the example of
being, by one's attitude toward life."[15] Put very simply,
how we pray is who we are.

3. In Prayer It Is Crucial to Be Present.
We Start Where We Are.

Merton wrote to Abdul Aziz that he places himself
"before God as if [he] saw Him."[16] Merton made himself present (a present?) to the present God. As he wrote
in *Spiritual Direction and Meditation,* ". . . I have to
withdraw my mind from all that prevents me from attending to God present in my heart."[17] Clearly this
principle is related to the first, that God is omnipresent,
and is also connected to the idea of listening discussed
in chapter 5. Prayer as attention of the whole person
God-ward requires that one detach from the myriad
distractions of daily life, distractions that are not only
external but internal, in the mind, the interior life. For
many the latter is more difficult than the former, difficult as *it* is in our wireless-oriented age. When one finds
geographic silence, one must still the almost constant
racket of the hyperactive human mind.

15. Shannon, ed., *Hidden Ground*, 367.
16. Shannon, ed., *Hidden Ground*, 63.
17. Merton, *Spiritual Direction and Meditation*, 68–69.

Before he left for Asia, Thomas Merton gave conferences at the Redwoods Monastery to a group of monastics interested in renewal and prayer.[18] Happily, Br.
David Steindl-Rast, OSB, kept and published his notes
on the conferences. (There will be more on these and
on the Alaskan and Asian conferences in the next chapter.) Br. David noted that "to start where you are and
to become aware of the connections—that was Thomas
Merton's approach to prayer."[19] Br. David continues his
report on Merton's teaching: "In prayer we discover
what we already have. You start where you are and you
deepen what you already have, and you realize that you
are already there. We already have everything, but we
don't know it and we don't experience it. Everything
has been given to us in Christ. All we need is to experience what we already possess." "If we really want
prayer," Merton said, "we'll have to give it time. We
must slow down to a human tempo."[20] Prayer requires
what monastic life is organized to give: stability that

18. See Merton's journal entries for October 8, 11, and 13, 1968.
The Other Side of the Mountain, The Journals of Thomas Merton,
vol. 7: *1967–1968*, ed. Patrick Hart (San Francisco: HarperSan-
Francisco, 1999), 199–201.

19. David Steindl-Rast, "Man of Prayer," in *Thomas Merton,
Monk: A Monastic Tribute*, ed. Patrick Hart (New York: Sheed &
Ward, 1974), 80.

20. Steindl-Rast, "Man of Prayer," 80, 81.

requires remaining and being "where one is." The life is arranged with time for prayer and, in a healthy community, life at a human tempo.

4. Two Difficulties Are Distractions and Self-Consciousness.

For Merton prayer is attentiveness to the presence of God, which is a gift given in the present moment. This is not easy since most of us are not where we are. We are "somewhere else," in regret about the past, or anxiety about the future, or attending to someone or something in a little box that draws us away from the person and place where our body is. These are huge hindrances to prayer. Mostly they are external, and we have, if we will exert it, control over most of them. The more difficult hindrances for many of us are internal. The most serious theologically is the inability to surrender to the grace given of prayer. The other is the almost ubiquitous problem of distractions.

Distractions are the thoughts that fill our heads and hearts when we attempt to pray. They are inevitable, but we must not give them energy by "fighting" them. At the outset the language of "fighting" is, itself, inappropriate for a discussion of prayer. It reflects a pugilistic rather than a receptive attitude, "against" rather than "accept." Why do we "fight" for justice? Or "hit" a button instead of pressing or tapping it? As well as our prayer, our unexamined, idiomatic use of language reveals who we are. In any case, Merton's advice is that we simply accept distractions and not worry overmuch about them.

From September 18 to 21, 1968, Merton gave conferences for the Sisters of the Precious Blood in Eagle River, Alaska. Several of them addressed prayer in very practical terms. He suggested complete absence of distraction was impossible. "The thing to do," he said, "is not to exclude everything but to bring it all in." "What do you do with distractions? You either simply let them pass by and ignore them, or you let them pass by and be perfectly content to have them. If you don't pay attention to them, the distractions don't remain." "If you don't wrestle with distractions . . . and just let them go by . . . they get less and less, and after a while there is nothing much left."[21] I am reminded of another (perhaps apocryphal?) story of a young novice who came to St. Teresa of Avila to report that the Blessed Virgin Mary was appearing to her in choir. The saint responded, "Just ignore her, dear, and she'll go away."

In fact, troubles with distraction are often linked to *self-consciousness.* Merton alluded to this in the Aziz letter with the Arabic term *fana,* annihilation or extinction. It is a sort of Islamic parallel to the Christian notion

21. Robert E. Daggy, ed., *Thomas Merton in Alaska* (New York: New Directions, 1988), 138, 139.

of *kenosis*, self-emptying, which we discussed earlier in this book. Practically, self-consciousness manifests as the obstacle of being present to ourselves in prayer, watching ourselves as we pray, often to see if we're "doing it right." It is a particular problem in meditation or wordless forms of prayer. Prayer is not about the person who prays. It is about God. The one who prays must set ego aside, "empty" self in order to receive God and return to God the gift of prayer that has been given. (Another reason the Buddhist concept of emptiness was so important to Merton was its existential application to the life of prayer.) Merton wrote to Aziz, "If I am still present 'myself' this is recognized as an obstacle."[22] The idea here is rooted in Merton's notion of God/Christ *within* as the source of authentic identity. If God/Christ is resident *within*, prayer must be primarily a resting in that Presence, setting aside the False Self and its distractions in order to reside in the True.

Writing again to his friend Etta Gullick (working with the formation of Anglican ordinands), Merton said that we must not worry overmuch about making "progress in prayer": " '[H]ow to make progress' is a good way to make people too aware of themselves. In the long run I think progress in prayer comes from the Cross and humiliation and whatever makes us really

22. Shannon, ed., *Hidden Ground*, 64.

experience our total poverty and nothingness, and also gets our mind off ourselves."[23] That "life is either all spiritual or not spiritual at all"[24] was one of Merton's most fundamental ideas. As he wrote to Aziz, we must wait for God to remove the obstacles to our prayer and not struggle overmuch with them ourselves. This only makes things worse, as we always do when we rush in to fix things that are really in God's job description. In the spiritual life obedience (recall chapter 5), surrender, receptivity, and waiting are critical and, for most of us, difficult.

5. Intentionally and Potentially All of Life Is Prayer.

If God is Emmanuel, with us, and if, as Merton asserts, prayer is turning completely toward God within in the present moment, then it *is* possible, as Paul suggested to the Thessalonians, to "pray ceaselessly" (1 Thess 5:17). Merton wrote to Gullick, "What I object to about 'the Spiritual Life,' is the fact that it is a part, a section, set off as if it were a whole. It is an aberration to set off our 'prayer' . . . from the rest of

23. Shannon, ed., *Hidden Ground*, 357.

24. Thomas Merton, *Thoughts in Solitude* (New York: Farrar, Straus & Giroux, 1958/1977), 56.

our existence as if we were sometimes spiritual, some-times not."[25] The distinction between "ordinary life" and the life of prayer is a false one. Not only must we pray as we are, but we *are* as we pray. Merton's plea is always for the unification, the congruence of all of life. Chapter 12 of *Thoughts in Solitude* opens, "If you want to have a spiritual life you must unify your life. A life is either all spiritual or not spiritual at all. No man can serve two masters. Your life is shaped by the end you live for. You are made in the image of what you desire."[26] (More on that last point in chapter 9.)

Concluding Thoughts

Merton wrote in *Contemplation in a World of Action*, "The real purpose of prayer . . . is the deepening of personal realization in love, the awareness of God."[27] Merton suggests we are already *in* prayer, *in* God. We must, so to speak, wake up to that reality. He wrote to Abdul Aziz that in centering "entirely on attention to the presence of God and to His will and His love," directly "seeking . . . the Face of the

25. Shannon, ed., *Hidden Ground*, 376.

26. Merton, *Thoughts in Solitude*, 56.

27. Quoted in *Thomas Merton: Essential Writings*, ed. Christine M. Bochen (Maryknoll, NY: Orbis Books, 2000), 86.

Invisible,"[28] one can, indeed, be "made [or remade] in the image of what we desire."[29] It is this toward which Merton's most mature teaching on prayer points. It is this wholehearted seeking that bridges the life of the monastic and of the serious Christian. Both desire to be more like God (or the Christ) who is both the object of desire and resident within. It is as Olive Wyon (quoted at the outset of this chapter) noted: "All our prayer . . . consists in wanting God"[30] and wanting to be more like God—that is, made in the image of what we desire. "What you have to do," Merton teaches, "is have this deeper consciousness of here I am and here is God and here are all these things which all belong to God. He and I and they are all involved in one love and everything manifests his goodness. Everything that I experience really reaches Him in some way or other. Nothing is an obstacle. He is in everything."[31] This is both our comfort and our challenge. Whoever we are, wherever we are in life's journey, the call is to be open to finding God in everything and everybody. If we do, or even *try* to do so, life will never, ever be boring.

28. Shannon, ed., *Hidden Ground*, 63, 64.
29. Merton, *Thoughts in Solitude*, 56.
30. Wyon, *Prayer*, 118.
31. Daggy, ed. *Thomas Merton in Alaska*, 140.

Chapter 8

Merton's Principles of Prayer (Part 2)[1]

On September 10, 1968, Merton left the Abbey of Our Lady of Gethsemani for the west coast. On October 15 he left for Asia, his final journey and, though he did not know it, his *transitus*. The talks that Merton gave in the intervening month contain his last and some of his richest teachings on prayer. The material is informal and unsystematic, often responses to questions, but no less important for that. In what follows we shall briefly visit his Alaskan conferences and his teachings to monastics gathered specifically to hear him speak on prayer. They were hosted by the Cistercian women at

1. Some of this material appeared in my article " 'I Spoke Most of Prayer': Thomas Merton on the West Coast (11 Sept–15 Oct 1968)," *Merton Seasonal* 35, no. 3 (Fall 2010): 10–19. I am grateful to the editor for permission to use it again here.

their monastery in Redwoods, California, which Merton had visited previously. I will make passing reference to very informal conferences on prayer Merton gave in India, which he admitted were "basically from notes I'd used in Alaska and California with a few added notions about a possible *Indian* contribution to a renewal of the Catholic Theology of Prayer" (italics in original).[2]

Because the material in the previous chapter was dense (and perhaps unfamiliar to some readers), you will find here some overlap. The echoes of ideas from the previous chapter as well as some repetition of quotations to underscore Merton's most important ideas are intentional.[3] Attentive readers will recognize again Merton's understanding of the True Self as fundamental to his insights about prayer. Think of these occasional recurrences as looking into the same room from different windows in order to receive different views of its contents.

2. Thomas Merton, *The Other Side of the Mountain*, The Journals of Thomas Merton, vol. 7: *1967–1968*, ed. Patrick Hart (San Francisco: HarperSanFrancisco, 1998), 297. Texts of two of the talks appear in Thomas Merton, "Two Conferences on Prayer: India 1968," *The Merton Annual* 31 (2018): 17–40.

3. Most of the quotations are from Robert E. Daggy, ed., *Thomas Merton in Alaska* (New York: New Directions, 1989) or Br. David Steindl-Rast, "Man of Prayer," in *Thomas Merton, Monk: A Monastic Tribute*, ed. Patrick Hart (New York: Sheed & Ward, 1974), which was originally published as "Recollections of Thomas Merton's Last Days in the West," *Monastic Studies* 7 (1969). References to Daggy's work appear in the text as TMA and to Steindl-Rast's as TMM.

The Alaskan Conferences

Between September 18 and 21 Merton spoke three times on prayer, twice to sisters and once to priests.[4] (Because it is quoted extensively, references to *Thomas Merton in Alaska* appear in the text as TMA.) The talks reflect a synthesis of Merton's wide reading and draw heavily on St. Paul, Sufism,[5] and the fourth-century Desert Christians, all of which were, at this point in his life, "go to" sources. The material circles around prayer and identity (what in chapter 2 was introduced as "understanding of the self"), prayer and freedom, and practical advice.

1. Prayer and Identity

Merton said "prayer and identity go together" (TMA 129) and used the existentialist term "alienation" to describe the absence of prayerfulness. An alienated person is one who isn't allowed to be herself, who is dominated by others' ideas (that is, she lives from the False Self). Contemplatives escape this alienation

4. The talks were published in numbers of *Sisters Today* 42 (1970–71) and in *The Priest* 42 (July–August 1986) as well as in Daggy's *Thomas Merton in Alaska* mentioned in note 3 above.

5. See also Bonnie Thurston, "Islam in Alaska: Sufi Material in *Thomas Merton in Alaska*," *The Merton Seasonal* 29, no. 4 (Spring 2005), 3–8, and Kathleen Witkowska Tarr's memoir, *We Are All Poets Here: Thomas Merton's 1968 Journey to Alaska—A Shared Story about Spiritual Seeking* (Anchorage, AK: VP&D House, 2017).

because contemplation "is really simple openness to God at every moment, and deep peace" (TMA 143). In an Indian conference to sisters Merton noted that "for us [religious and contemplatives] there is no identity crisis because our identity is found in our response to Christ." He continued, "[T]he ground of identity is the sense of having been chosen by Christ."[6] "[O]ur prayer, as obedience, is the fruit of Christ's obedience; and it is union with Christ's obedience."[7] "Prayer . . . is essentially an act of surrender to God's love."[8] In the Alaska conferences Merton noted that, at the center, one experiences God's love and mercy, and as a result one prays "with your whole life" (TMA 129). "[T]he real meaning of our life is to develop people who really love God and who radiate love. . . . For that they have to be fully unified and fully themselves" (TMA 149). That is, persons must become and be their True Selves, the selves in whom God and Christ have been interiorized or, perhaps more accurately, discovered.

Far from separating one from others, deep prayer unites, with God and with other human beings. Merton described to Jesuit scholastics in India Christ "so interiorized in me that He and I are one and my prayer is therefore His prayer. . . . The theology of prayer must

6. Merton, "Two Conferences on Prayer," 23.
7. Merton, "Two Conferences on Prayer," 29.
8. Merton, "Two Conferences on Prayer," 28.

take account of the point at which Our Lord as a . . . separate object vanishes."[9] With regard to prayer and others Merton noted in Alaska, "When I pray, I am, in a certain sense, everybody. The mind that prays in me is more than my own mind, and the thoughts that come up . . . are more than my own thoughts because this deep consciousness when I pray is a place of encounter between myself and God and between the common love of everybody" (TMA 135). "When I pray the Church prays in me" (TMA 134). The individual at prayer is the *Church* at prayer. (Thus an early Church council concluded that we may pray the *Our* Father alone.) This awareness is another way that alienation is overcome and another way that monasticism is *not* "fleeing the world." (See chapter 4.)

2. Prayer and Freedom

For Merton, prayer has to be carried out in freedom. "It isn't a question of there being one right way to pray . . . we should be perfectly free to explore all sorts of avenues and ways of prayer" (TMA 81). Merton was basically opposed to the use of prayer manuals and mechanical formulas of prayer and suggested that people develop a spirit of freedom in the life of prayer (TMA 78). "[P]rayer is our real freedom" (TMA 113).

9. Merton, "Two Conferences on Prayer," 38 and 39.

Merton asserts, "This is what Christ came on earth for, to give people this kind of freedom, this kind of simplicity" (TMA 141). Behind Merton's statement one hears echoes of St. Paul: "For freedom Christ has set us free. Stand firm, therefore, and do not submit again to a yoke of slavery" (Gal 5:1). (I recall a saying I heard attributed to Toni Morrison: "The function of freedom is to free someone else.") Too rigid adherence to some "method" of prayer can be "a yoke of slavery" and imprison the spiritual life. Merton suggests that "the only rule that there is in prayer is that you never say anything you don't mean" (TMA 119). The more one lives from knowledge of God resident within, from the True Self, the greater freedom there is in prayer—and in life.

3. Practical Advice

Merton's Alaskan conferences combined spiritual psychology and theology. He gave down-to-earth advice like "be honest, don't say in prayer what you don't mean. . . . You don't get to God through a system. You speak from your heart" (TMA 118). He spoke about distraction in prayer (which was introduced in the previous chapter), saying, "The thing to do is not to exclude everything but to bring it all in. Try to realize that distractions go away if you have time for them to go away." This is an important reminder that prayer requires time, dare I say "leisure." "If you don't pay any attention to them, the distractions don't remain" (TMA 138).

Our Lady of the Redwoods, California

Redwoods was a foundation of Belgian Trappistines. At the times of Merton's visits M. Myriam Dardenne was the superior. Merton related well to these women, many of whom were of European formation. He had visited them once before, May 7 to 14, 1968, and that visit is recorded in the beautifully produced *Woods, Shore, Desert*, which reproduces Merton's photographs.[10] Merton returned to the Redwoods on October 11 for a three-day conference on the contemplative life with a gathering of men and women religious who had specifically asked him to speak about prayer. (Again, because there are so many references to *Thomas Merton, Monk* they appear in the text as "TM Monk.")

According to Br. David Steindl-Rast, whose notes preserved the essential material in Merton's conferences, "To start where you are and to become aware of connections . . . was Thomas Merton's approach to prayer" (TM Monk 80). "In prayer we discover what we already have. You start where you are and you deepen what you already have, and you realize you are already

10. Thomas Merton, *Woods, Shore, Desert* (Santa Fe: Museum of New Mexico Press, 1982).

there" (TM Monk 80). In addition to identity and freedom, as did the Alaska conferences, these talks warned
specifically against imposition of rigid forms of prayer.
"The real contemplative standard," Merton said, "is
to have no standard, to just be yourself. That's what
God is asking of us, to be ourselves" (TM Monk 83).
This, of course, is very practical advice, since everyone
else is taken.

In light of the changes that had recently been pro-
posed for religious orders by Vatican II, it is not sur-
prising that Merton addressed religious institutions
and prayer.[11] "The institution must serve the development of the individual person. . . . What we need are
person-centered communities, not institution-centered
ones" (TM Monk 85). "[W]hy did any of us become
religious if we didn't want to pray?" (TM Monk 84).
Forms of prayer, especially rigidly imposed ones, can
hinder authentic prayer. Anyone, monastic or otherwise, who prays the Offices or "set" meditations knows
"saying prayers" is not necessarily always praying. The

---

11. He addressed the same subject in talks both to the Loretto
community near Gethsemani and to meetings he had with contem-
plative prioresses at Gethsemani. For more, see Thomas Merton,
The Springs of Contemplation, ed. Jane Marie Richardson (New
York: Farrar, Straus & Giroux, 1992), and *Hidden in the Same
Mystery: Thomas Merton and Loretto*, gen. ed. Bonnie Thurston,
Loretto ed. Sr. Mary Swain (Louisville, KY: Fons Vitae Press, 2010).

words can be "said" while the mind and heart are elsewhere. Merton's advice is to "discover what is useful
. . . then discard structures that don't help, and keep
structures that do help" (TM Monk 85). How this
might be effected in a monastic community with a life
built on the Hours Merton doesn't say. Although he
does at several points in his journals describe how he
himself struggled to pray in choir, he does not at any
point *condemn* the pattern of community Offices or the
monastic *horarium*.

In fact, the external structures of monastic life do
not figure highly in the last talks Merton gave on monasticism. Those talks appear in *The Asian Journal of
Thomas Merton* as "Thomas Merton's View of Monasticism" and "Marxism and Monastic Perspectives." In
the latter (to which earlier reference was made in this
book) he quoted a Tibetan monk about to be driven
from his monastery. "He sent a message to a nearby
abbot friend . . . 'What do we do?' The abbot sent
back a strange message . . . 'From now on, Brother, everybody stands on his own feet.' "[12] Merton called this
"very significant" and noted that "we can no longer rely
on being supported by structures that may be destroyed
at any moment. . . . You cannot rely on structures.

12. *The Asian Journal of Thomas Merton*, ed. N. Burton, P. Hart,
and J. Laughlin (New York: New Directions, 1973), 338.

The time for relying on structures has disappeared."[13] As institutional structures change or are destroyed, it is the individual who has developed his or her own deep and authentic prayer that will preserve the monastic charism, perhaps Christianity, itself. Spoken in 1968, Merton's seems a timely reminder.

In any case, Merton reminded his fellow contemplatives at Redwoods that prayer takes time:

> If we really want prayer, we'll have to give it time. We must slow down to a human tempo. . . .The reason why we don't take time is a feeling that we have to keep moving. This is a real sickness. . . .We live in the fullness of time. Every moment is God's own good time. . . . The whole thing boils down to giving ourselves in prayer a chance to realize that we have what we seek. We don't have to rush after it. It is there all the time, and if we give it time it will make itself known to us. (TM Monk 81)

Merton again spoke of honesty in prayer and reminded his hearers that intercessory prayer is the way we express love for people. "What truly matters is not how to get the most out of life," he said, "but how to recollect yourself so that you can fully give yourself" (TM Monk 83). This recalls something Merton had written in *New Seeds of Contemplation*:

13. Merton, *The Asian Journal*, 338.

I shall discover who I am and shall possess my true identity by losing myself in [God].
    And that is what is called sanctity.[14]

Concluding Thoughts

Perhaps the reason Merton's writing continues to be so popular, that he still serves many as a spiritual guide, is because of the clarity and attractiveness of his teaching on prayer and contemplation, terms that are used almost synonymously in his work. As noted in the previous chapter, for Merton "prayer" was not narrowly defined by intercessory prayer or any particular method of praying but was a more comprehensive, indeed, *encompassing* term approaching what was meant by "mind" (habitual disposition) in the Philippians hymn we examined earlier. While Merton wrote as a monk and his thought on these matters was formed in the monastery, it is remarkably accessible to people who seek a more profound spiritual life. I close these two chapters on prayer—which is, of course, the heart of Christian as well as monastic spirituality—by lifting up a few ideas under the categories of nonduality, simplicity, and temporality that for me summarize Merton's thoughts on prayer.

14. Thomas Merton, *New Seeds of Contemplation* (New York: New Directions, 1961/1972), 63.

Nonduality

Merton stresses nonduality in prayer, by which he means there should be little difference between life and prayer. Daily life and prayer are not separate. "Prayer" is not a subset of "activities." Merton notes, "The spiritual life is first of all a *life*" (italics in original). "If we want to be spiritual, then let us first of all live our lives."[15] Prayer is not a subcategory of things to *do*. Prayer is who we were created to *be*. How I pray is who I am, and there should be no duality between my life and God's life in me. "God utters me like a word containing a partial thought of Himself."[16] This, of course, echoes the teaching of Evagrius and several Fathers of Eastern Christianity who thought human beings originated in and to some extent shared the mind of God. It is another subject for another time, but one often hears echoes of Orthodox thought in Merton's teaching on prayer.[17]

15. Thomas Merton, *Thoughts in Solitude* (New York: Farrar, Straus & Giroux/Noonday, 1956/1977), 46–47.

16. Merton, *New Seeds of Contemplation*, 37.

17. Rowan Williams has made significant contributions to our understanding of Merton's thought about Eastern Orthodoxy. See, for example, his *A Silent Action: Engagements with Thomas Merton* (Louisville, KY: Fons Vitae Press, 2011) and Bernadette Dieker and Jonathan Montaldo, eds., *Merton and Hesychasm: The Prayer of the Heart* (Louisville, KY: Fons Vitae Press, 2003).

Prayer overcomes duality because the one who prays is united with who and what is prayed for and, fundamentally, to Whom intercession is made. Prayer "is a place of encounter between myself and God and between the common love of everybody" (TMA 135). "I must look for my identity," Merton writes, "not only in God but in other men."[18] The Christian's authentic identity in God and in prayer leads him or her, not into isolation, but into community, "with-ness" to all that God created, keeps in being, and loves. As Merton told the Jesuit scholastics in India, "There is no theology of prayer that is not also a theology of compassion."[19] Thus the gift of prayer is not only for the individual to whom it is given. "God does not give us graces or talents or virtues for ourselves alone. We are members one of another and everything that is given to one member is given for the whole body."[20] One hears again St. Paul's influence on Merton's thought: spiritual gifts and graces, like that of prayer, are given "for the common good" (1 Cor 12:7), the "body."

Simplicity

Merton teaches that one reason we have troubles in prayer is that we make such a big fuss out of something

18. Merton, *New Seeds of Contemplation*, 51.
19. Merton, "Two Conferences on Prayer," 32.
20. Merton, *New Seeds of Contemplation*, 56.

that is essentially very simple. He explained to the Indian sisters that "[p]rayer is simply nothing else but . . . being in God's presence and being known to God and responding to Him in the best way we can, praying as we can."[21] Mostly, simply to pray is "to start where you are and to become aware of connections" (TM Monk 80). It is dangerous and distracting to create too many rigid methods and rules around prayer, which is really essentially alertness and aliveness in the present moment, openness to the omnipresence of God. This might be to say that prayer gets complex when we make our definition of prayer too narrow. Then we worry if we are "doing it right," which leads to self-consciousness, a fatal error because prayer is centered on and "about" God, not the one who prays or, in intercessory prayer, the matter prayed for. And if prayer is openness to and awareness of God's love at the root of all that is, how *can* we "get it wrong"? How could God's love, the root of Being, the *primum mobile*, be wrong? Thoreau's command to "Simplify! Simplify!" seems, in a way, to summarize this aspect of Merton's teaching on prayer.

Temporality

The truth is that prayer requires time. Because our identity *is* prayer, it's pretty clear that we were made

---

21. Merton, "Two Conferences on Prayer," 24.

for eternity. Praying exercises our eternity. In the disordered culture in which we live, if we are to become who we are, paradoxically, we begin to uncover our identity by consistently practicing some form, even method (!), of prayer. Eventually, for many, the method is left behind and pure prayer remains. One abandons the container for the contents, the mode of transport for the journey itself. We have to give the "practice" of prayer priority. In one of the Alaskan conferences Merton said that hurried prayer leads to distractions.

Whether we realize it or not, how we use our time is a clear indication of our real identity. Tragically, even devout Christians sometimes don't seem to know how much God loves them or they would want to be with God more frequently. People who "don't have time to pray" don't yet know who they are, don't know they are "partial thoughts of God," perhaps don't even realize that a lot of their lives already *is* prayer. The seventeenth-century English poet George Herbert addressed just this point in his poem "The Elixir": "Teach me, my God and King, / In all things thee to see, / And what I do in any thing, / To do it as for thee."[22] And one remembers Br. Lawrence, he of *The Practice of the Presence of God*, who said he was as close to God in the kitchen washing pots as at the altar rail.

22. *The Works of George Herbert*, ed. F. E. Hutchinson (Oxford: Clarendon Press, 1941/1972), 184.

Finally, Merton himself said, "[N]othing that anyone says will be that important. The great thing is prayer. Prayer itself. If you want a life of prayer, the way to get it is by praying" (TM Monk 70). "[L]et things alone and give yourself time and [be] patient and attentive and open to God" (TMA 140). As he was leaving for Asia, speaking to a gathering of fellow religious seeking renewal through prayer, Merton asked rhetorically, "What do we want, if not to pray? O.K., now, pray" (TM Monk 84). And then he asked the more profound question, and the one that applies to us all, monastic or not: "What is keeping us back from lives of prayer? Perhaps we don't really want to pray. This is the thing we have to face" (TM Monk 85).

Chapter 9

"The End You Live For"

In John's gospel a question that suggests a Christology of open-endedness frames the ministry of Jesus. In fact, John's story of Jesus begins and ends with essentially the same question. In chapter 1, as the disciples of John the Baptist see Jesus, he asks them, "What are you looking for?" (1:38). In chapter 18, as those same disciples watch, Judas and the detachment of soldiers enter the garden, and Jesus steps forward and twice says, "Whom are you looking for?" (18:4 and 7), the same question he asks the grieving Magdalene by the empty tomb (20:15).[1] "What are you looking for?" "Whom seek ye?" (Those words of the older translation echo in my head to the music of Bach's *St. John Passion*.) These

---

1. With the exception of changes in number and gender of the pronoun and corresponding change in the verb, the question is essentially the same. The verb *zeteo* means to seek or search but also to strive for something.

are the fundamental questions of human life. When the basic necessities of life are in place, human beings seek for meaning. In one way or another, potential monastics are asked this question as they seek postulancy, and it undoubtedly arises, perhaps repeatedly, in the lives not only of monks but of thoughtful people in general.

Merton knew that "what are you looking for?" is a critical question. To ask it is to ask "what gives my life meaning?" "What is the goal toward which my life moves?" To frame the question in Teilhardian terms: "What is my 'omega point'?"[2] Toward what does everything in my life move? Or, to use Paul Tillich's term, what is my "ultimate concern," that for which I would abandon everything else? One of the many books that appeared in 2018 to celebrate the quinquagenary of Merton's birth was *What I Am Living For*, a collection edited by Jon M. Sweeney of reflections by a wide range of spiritual writers and practitioners that address this very question.[3]

---

2. We know Merton knew the work of Teilhard de Chardin. Two articles he wrote on the Jesuit appear in *Love and Living*, ed. Naomi Burton Stone and Patrick Hart (New York: Farrar, Straus, Giroux, 1979). Merton quipped to sisters in India, "The only thing that a censor has finally stopped on me was an article on Teilhard de Chardin." Thomas Merton, "Two Conferences on Prayer," *The Merton Annual* 31 (2018): 29.

3. Jon M. Sweeney, ed., *What I Am Living For* (Notre Dame, IN: Ave Maria Press, 2018).

Merton wrote in *Thoughts in Solitude*, "Your life is shaped by the end you live for. You are made in the image of what you desire."[4] Ultimately, desire has to do with volition, what we choose. God chose some people for monastic life, but they had to choose monastic life for themselves. This pattern of *being* chosen and accepting/choosing that for which one is chosen characterizes all Christian vocation, as, indeed, it characterized the life of Mary, the mother of Jesus. In *Basic Principles of Monastic Spirituality* Merton opens the chapter "Spouse of Christ" with this sobering reminder: "We are not contemplatives by the mere fact of living an enclosed and penitential life. We can indeed be more active, more restless and more distracted in the cloister than we would be in the active life."[5] In short, the cloister and the habit do not a monastic make. Some deeper response is called for. It may well be choosing what God desires for us.

From a different angle, we are now reprising the theme of identity that was raised earlier in chapter 3 and has echoed through the book. It was also the central theme of a retreat given by Bernardo Bonowitz, OCSO, to the Brazilian Thomas Merton Society in October

---

4. Thomas Merton, *Thoughts in Solitude* (New York: Farrar, Straus & Giroux/Noonday, 1956/1977), 56.

5. Thomas Merton, *Basic Principles of Monastic Spirituality* (Springfield, IL: Templegate Publishers, 1957/1996), 89.

2014. The talks were published in *Cistercian Studies Quarterly* in 2015. Therein Bonowitz notes that "no one can rescue himself from being a false self."[6] God is the source of our true identity. "By the inestimable gift of liberty with which God has endowed us, he had given us . . . the responsibility to decide how we will answer the question which we are." We "participate in the creation of one's own self" through our response, "the progressive, transforming welcome of God into one's own life."[7]

Whether recognized or not, the deepest human desire is for God who is the source of the True Self. In July 2019 the Jesuits in Britain offered an online experience of thirty-one days with St. Ignatius. The July 3 reflection included two statements by Brian Purfield that are very relevant to what we are considering. "For Ignatius, our deepest longing is identical with the will of God." "Ignatius was convinced that we must find this will of God in our own hearts. Our deepest and most authentic desire is the point at which we are most united with God."[8]

6. Bernardo Bonowitz, "Reaping Where Merton Has Sown: A Retreat for the Merton Centenary," *Cistercian Studies Quarterly* 50, no. 1 (2015): 43.

7. Bonowitz, "Reaping Where Merton Has Sown," 45.

8. Copied from the July 3, 2019, reflection by Brian Purfield in the "31 Days of St. Ignatius" series offered by the Jesuits in Britain on Pathwaystogod.org. I am grateful for permission to use it here.

What we desire tells us who we are. What we desire is often what we love. Again in *Thoughts in Solitude* Merton says, "[T]he things that we love tell us what we are."[9] In order to know what we *really* desire, we have to know who we *really* are. We must shatter the image of who we tell ourselves we are and know ourselves more accurately and intimately. In a talk presented at New Clairvaux Abbey (subsequently printed in *Cistercian Studies Quarterly*), on Thomas Merton, St. Bernard, and the prophetic dimension of monasticism, Ephrem Arcement, OSB, notes, "Cenobitic monasticism is, at least in part, based upon the conviction that transformation happens in community—through the confrontation of one's limited self with another's. . . . Presence fosters encounter, which, in turn, fosters transformation."[10]

Similarly, Merton wrote in "The Spiritual Father in the Desert Tradition," "The monk does not come into the desert to reinforce his own ego-image, but to be delivered from it. After all, this worship of the self is the last and most difficult of idolatries to detect and get rid of."[11] This is undoubtedly one of the "severe

9. Merton, *Thoughts in Solitude*, 22.

10. Ephrem Arcement, OSB, "Thomas Merton, Saint Bernard, and the Prophetic Dimension of Monasticism in the Early Twenty-First Century," *Cistercian Studies Quarterly* 51, no. 4 (2016): 457.

11. Thomas Merton, "The Spiritual Father in the Desert Tradition," in *Contemplation in a World of Action* (Garden City, NY: Doubleday/Image, 1973), 298.

mercies" (to use a term associated with C. S. Lewis) of community life. You can't live for very long with other people, in a monastery or in a family, and not have your own image of yourself knocked around a bit. In fact, it is often only in community or in trusting relationships that our fingers can be pried away from their clutch on our own view of ourselves. Writing of St. Benedict in *The Silent Life* Merton said, "The essence of the rule of St. Benedict is the renunciation of self-will in imitation of Christ."[12] "Renunciation of self-will" on the part of the individual builds community and forwards one's own spiritual journey. In his retreat talks Bonowitz asserted that "the only way of unmasking and unmaking the false self and being introduced to the true self is through detachment."[13]

A primary detachment must be from what we do, because who we are is not what we do. Often our image of ourselves is related to our work, our missions, what we do. To avoid that very real trap, which is set in any number of ways with several luscious lures by our society, we might regularly ask ourselves, "Who am I when no one else is around?" "When I go into my cell/ my room and close the door and wait for the cell to teach me everything, what does my cell say about me?" If accepted and not kept at bay, periods of silence and

12. Thomas Merton, *The Silent Life* (New York: Farrar, Straus & Giroux, 1957/1981), 65.
13. Bonowitz, "Reaping Where Merton Has Sown," 49.

solitude help one answer this crucial question. Merton wrote at length about the importance of the cell in section 2 of "The Case for Eremitism," part 2 of *Contemplation in a World of Action*. The "most important 'ascetic practice,'" Merton wrote, "is solitude itself, and 'sitting' alone in the silence of the cell."[14] (See related material on solitude in chapter 6.)

Periods of solitude help one to remove her masks and confront who she is as opposed to what she does. Merton wrote that "the monastic life is a *search for God* and not a mission to accomplish this or that work." "Each of us will find God in his own way, but all of us together will find Him by living together in the Spirit, in perfect charity, as members of one another in Christ, recognizing the fact that Christ lives in us both as a community and as individuals" (italics in original).[15]

Here is a story Merton includes in *Wisdom of the Desert* about individuation and desire:

> A Brother asked one of the elders: What good thing shall I do, and have life thereby? The old man replied: God alone knows what is good. However, I have heard it said that someone inquired of Father Abbot Nisteros the great, the friend of Abbot Anthony, asking: What good work shall I do? and that he replied:

14. Merton, "The Cell," in *Contemplation in a World of Action*, 265.

15. Merton, *Basic Principles*, 100.

Not all works are alike. For Scripture says that Abraham was hospitable and God was with him. Elias loved solitary prayer, and God was with him. And David was humble, and God was with him. Therefore, whatever you see your soul to desire according to God, do that thing, and you shall keep your heart safe.[16]

"Our true self," Merton wrote in *The Silent Life*, "is the person we are meant to be."[17] David was not meant to be Abraham, nor Abraham Elias. Each person is to become himself or herself. In part 1 of *Contemplation in a World of Action* on Monastic Renewal, essay 3 is "The Identity Crisis," which Merton calls "a grave problem in America" and proceeds to diagnose as a serious societal illness. One doesn't receive identity with biological life; "one must create [identity] for himself by choices that are significant."[18] Identity "means having a belief one stands by . . . having certain definite ways of responding to life. . . . In this sense, identity is one's witness to truth in one's life."[19]

So after, in the context of a community that forces one to be honest with oneself and control self-will, one

16. Thomas Merton, *The Wisdom of the Desert: Sayings from the Desert Fathers of the Fourth Century* (New York: New Directions, 1960), 25–26.

17. Merton, *The Silent Life*, 22.

18. Merton, *Contemplation in a World of Action*, 78.

19. Merton, *Contemplation in a World of Action*, 78.

has worked to follow Plato's great injunction to "know thyself," after one has some accurate knowledge of his strengths and weaknesses, where the hidden warts and wounds are, then the dust is sufficiently cleared away for him to examine his *authentic* and *honest* desires, the desires that, whether one is conscious of them or not, are forming one in their image. Merton suggests that "to unify your life unify your desires. To spiritualize your life spiritualize your desires."[20]

I suspect that some of us think of "desire" in terms similar to how the missionary lady Rose Sayer (brilliantly and hilariously played by Katherine Hepburn in the 1951 film *The African Queen*) thought of human nature. "Human nature is what we are put in this world to rise above,"[21] she opines. I suspect some folks think the point of monastic observances is to whack the desire out of us. But desire is not evil. For example, if there were no sexual desire, there would be no human beings. Monastic life is not to obliterate but to clarify and elevate human desires. Monasteries are places where human desires are purified, or, perhaps more accurately, resurrected, made new, perfected. Whatever else resurrection life is, I suspect that in it all that is partial or broken in us will be perfected and healed.

20. Merton, *Thoughts in Solitude*, 56.
21. I am paraphrasing from memory, having seen the film at least half a dozen times.

Unfortunately "desire" is a word that has been coopted by writers about sexuality. A little etymology dispels that (pardon the word) misconception. Neither of the words usually translated from the Greek New Testament into English as "desire" have an essentially sexual connotation. *Eudokia* means "choice" or "choosing." And *thelema* means "wish" or "desire." Wait until you hear what the Latin root means! The English word "desire" comes from the Latin *desiderare*. In Latin texts it means "to long for something absent." Its root, *sidereus* (from *sidus, sideris,* "heavenly body") means "of the stars." To desire is, in fact, to long for something absent, something that is "from the heavens," something that lightens the darkness of the night, and then to choose it.

In 1994 Philip Sheldrake (then SJ) published an important book called *Befriending Our Desires.* Sheldrake suggests, "Desires are best understood as our most honest experiences of ourselves, in all our complexity and depth, as we relate to people and things around us."[22] Sheldrake writes that our desires speak to us of what we do not have and therefore they are a condition of openness to possibility and to the future.[23] In this process, "the arrival at what is new . . . cannot be complete until the ending of the previous life structure

22. Philip Sheldrake, *Befriending Our Desires* (Notre Dame, IN: Ave Maria Press, 1994), 12.

23. Sheldrake, *Befriending Our Desires*, 25.

is complete."[24] Relatedly, Merton teaches that the monastic vocation "is to live by the will of God in prayer and sacrifice. . . . We must never forget that we will not be able to do this unless we have really renounced the past."[25] The *creation* of identity by means of appropriate desire (choosing) is ultimately *cooperation* with Christ. "Behold!" declares Christ at the end of the Revelation to John, "I make all things new" (21:5). The Matthean Jesus hints at the same thing when he speaks of "the renewal of all things" (Matt 19:28). Christ does the work. We cooperate—or don't.

Desires are a condition of openness to the future. This is a wonderful gloss on Merton's statement that we are made in the image of what we desire. Monastic life orients us toward who we really are: people with a longing for God, a longing so intense that we choose the eternal longing over any temporal fulfillment. One literally longs for something from the heavens. And, as all that "coming down" language about Jesus in John's gospel and the Epistle to the Philippians suggests,[26] God meets that longing, not just in monastics, but in all maturing Christians. God comes down to raise us up. We long for the light that shines in darkness and that the darkness can never overcome. We long for the

24. Sheldrake, *Befriending Our Desires*, 113–14.
25. Merton, *Basic Principles*, 100, 101.
26. See, for example, John 3:31; 6:38, 50, 58; 8:23; and Philippians 2:6-8.

God whom we cannot possess but who possesses us and remakes us in the Divine image. Merton wrote, "The monastic life of humility, obedience, liturgical prayer, spiritual reading, penance, manual labour, contemplation tends to ever purify the soul of the monk and lead him to intimacy with Christ."[27] That desire for intimacy with Christ is what brought many monastics to the monastery in the first place and what many Christians desire.

Merton says our life is shaped by the end we live for. He also suggests we are made in the image of the God we worship. In this regard, a sobering passage in *No Man Is an Island* bears reproducing here:

> Every man becomes the image of the God he adores.
>
> He whose worship is directed to a dead thing becomes a dead thing.
>
> He who loves corruption rots.
>
> He who loves a shadow becomes . . . a shadow.
>
> He who loves things that must perish lives in dread of their perishing.
>
> The contemplative also, who seeks to keep God prisoner in his heart, becomes a prisoner within the narrow limits of his own heart. . . .
>
> The man who leaves the Lord the freedom of the Lord adores the Lord in His freedom and receives the liberty of the sons of God.

27. Merton, *Basic Principles*, 89.

This man loves like God and is carried away, the
captive of the Lord's invisible freedom.[28]

It is not only monastics who must continually ask
themselves "What do I desire *now*?" and "How will it
continue to shape me?" It is an appropriate extension
of Merton's intention in this teaching that all of us
who are Christian also ask, "What do I love *now*, and
how does it tell me who I am today?" Both Sheldrake's
sense of letting go of the past for the sake of what is new
in the future and Merton's insistence on continuing
conversio morum converge in the question, "How does
Love tell you what you are?" The more fully one sur-
renders to Love, the more perfectly one is conformed to
Love's image, to Jesus, God who is Love visible among
us. Thus it is, as St. Benedict wrote in the Prologue to
the Rule, "What, dear brothers, is more delightful than
this voice of the Lord calling to us? See how the Lord in
his love shows us the way of life. . . . [A]s we progress
in this way of life and in faith, we shall run on the path
of God's commandments, our hearts overflowing with
the inexpressible delight of love."[29]

28. Thomas Merton, *No Man Is an Island* (New York: Double-
day/Image, 1967), 179–80.
29. Timothy Fry, ed., *The Rule of St. Benedict* (Collegeville, MN:
Liturgical Press, 1981), 161, 165.

Chapter 10

Merton on Saying "Yes": Creative Consent[1]

As Monica Weis's book *Thomas Merton and the Celts* demonstrates, Merton's monastic thought and practice were influenced by the Celtic traditions of Christianity.[2] He gave talks to Gethsemani's novices on Celtic Christianity and monasticism in 1964, 1966, and 1967. One

---

1. Some material in this chapter was first published as Bonnie Thurston, " 'Creative Consent': Thomas Merton on Saying 'Yes,' " *The Merton Journal* 19, no. 1 (2012): 36–42. I am grateful that permission was given to use it here.

2. Monica Weis, *Thomas Merton and the Celts* (Eugene, OR: Pickwick Publications, 2016). Merton's secretary, Br. Patrick Hart, OCSO (of blessed memory), also did significant work on Celtic monasticism that is published in *The Merton Seasonal* 44, no. 2 (Summer 2019): 9–40. Merton scholar and director of the Thomas Merton Center at Bellarmine University, Paul M. Pearson, has also done important work on Merton and Celtic monasticism.

of the most important Celtic monastic establishments was the community that was founded on the island of Iona, a community that, in a different form, continues to flourish today. The story of Iona's revival and reconstruction after the First World War is worth pursuing.[3] The oldest continuously used chapel on the island today is St. Oran's. Traditionally, it was the burial place of the Scottish kings. The following poetic vignette describes something I saw in that chapel that is relevant to the subject of monastic assent, of "saying yes."

St. Oran's Chapel

In the oldest place
where kings are buried
the oldest woman,

bent and staggering,
fell onto the rickety back bench.
Bowed head, shoulders hunched,
face in hands, pink scalp
visible through thin, white hair,
she prayed and prayed and prayed.

3. For a thumbnail history, see the introductory note "The Iona Community," in *The Iona Community Worship Book*, 3rd ed. (Glasgow: Wild Goose Publications, 1994), and material in Bonnie Thurston, *Belonging to Borders: A Sojourn in the Celtic Tradition* (Collegeville, MN: Liturgical Press, 2011).

Then, abruptly, with youthful vigor,
sat up, said aloud, "Yes!"
rested peacefully a while longer,
after several minutes struggled up
chanting under her breath,
"yes, yes, yes."

In the oldest place
where commoners are resurrected,
the holiest word.[4]

Biblical/Theological Introduction

Christian theology teaches that God made human beings and endowed them with a radical freedom that they subsequently misused. We discussed that freedom in the context of the True and False Selves in chapters 3 and 9. But "in the fullness of time" (Gal 4:4), Mary's "yes," her *fiat* recorded by St. Luke (1:38), allowed God to set in motion a *re-creation*, signaled at the beginnings of Mark's and John's gospels with the carefully chosen Greek word *arche*, beginning. By saying "yes" to God's original intention in a world that had wandered from it, Mary inaugurated, and her Son gave, that world a new beginning. I suspect her own definite "yes" did the same for that woman in St. Oran's Chapel.

---

4. Thurston, *Belonging to Borders*, 39. I am grateful for permission to use the poem here.

The cross was Jesus' "yes" to God. The resurrection was God's "yes" to Jesus. In *Days of Awe and Wonder* Marcus Borg put it succinctly, "The powers of this world killed Jesus and God vindicated him, which is one of the central meanings of Easter."[5] St. Paul deeply understood the divine yes-saying and wrote to the Corinthians, "For . . . Jesus Christ, whom we proclaimed among you . . . was not 'Yes and No'; but in him it is always 'Yes.' For in him every one of God's promises is a 'Yes'" (2 Cor 1:19-20). In Jesus, every one of God's promises is "yes." The risen Christ is God's cosmic "yes." Ruth Burrows reminds us that "Jesus is not now 'yes' and now 'no' but always the eternal 'yes.'"[6] One's personal "yes" is crucial to monastic spirituality and Christian identity.

"Yes" and the True Self/Authentic Identity

Just as monastics respond to God's call with an affirmative response, we all have the opportunity to participate in our own "yes." Merton understood that at the heart of every one of us is potentially a corresponding

5. Marcus J. Borg, "The Heart and Soul of Christianity," in *Days of Awe and Wonder* (New York: HarperCollins/Harper One, 2017), 201.

6. Ruth Burrows, *Guidelines for Mystical Prayer* (Mahwah, NJ: Paulist Press, 1976, 2017), 140.

"yes." This "yes" is the substance and core of our True Self. We must not only uncover it but *choose* it as our basic life stance and response to God. Speaking to Jesuit scholastics in India, Merton described the mediatorship of Christ and said, "[T]here is a kind of interiorization that has to take place in prayer in which there is no longer I and the Mediator . . . in which the Mediator becomes so interiorized in me that He and I are one."[7] We can say "yes" to this, and our "creative consent" becomes our personal, resurrective *fiat*. As Benedict says in a slightly different context in the Prologue to the Rule, "[God] waits for us daily to translate into action . . . his holy teachings."[8] God waits for our response to the divine invitation. God awaits our invitation to take up residence within us, or, perhaps more accurately, waits for us to discover that residence within.

In this book we have often alluded to Merton's view of the True Self. This divinely given, authentic identity was for Merton God's utterance of the Divine Self within us. As he said so starkly in *New Seeds of Contemplation*, "Unless [God] utters Himself in you, speaks His own name in the center of your soul, you will no more know Him than a stone knows the ground upon

7. Thomas Merton, "Two Conferences on Prayer: India 1968," *The Merton Annual* 31 (2018): 36.

8. Timothy Fry, ed., *The Rule of St. Benedict* (Collegeville, MN: Liturgical Press, 1981), 163.

which it rests in its inertia."[9] This understanding of authentic identity became for Merton a point of contact among Orthodox Christianity, Sufism and Buddhism.[10] In what follows, I allude very briefly to this point of dialogue between Christianity and Islamic Sufism as it was treated in a talk by Sr. Mary Luke Tobin, SL (of blessed memory), at Nazareth College in Rochester, New York, in November 1990.[11]

Tobin summarized Merton's teaching by saying that the human person is a heart and a secret. The secret is God's, God's innermost knowledge of the person. And that secret

> is the word "yes." And the act of "yes." It is a secret affirmation which God places in my heart, a "yes" to God. That's God's secret. . . . My destiny in life

9. Thomas Merton, *New Seeds of Contemplation* (New York: New Directions, 1961), 39.

10. See, for example, Merton's essay, "Final Integration: Toward a 'Monastic Therapy,'" which was generated by Persian-American psychoanalyst A. Reza Arasteh's book *Final Integration in Adult Personality* (Leiden: Brill, 1965), first published in *Monastic Studies* 6 (1968): 87–88, and reprinted in *Contemplation in a World of Action* (Garden City, NY: Doubleday/Image, 1973), 219–31, and reprinted in *Thomas Merton: Selected Essays*, ed. Patrick F. O'Connell (Maryknoll, NY: Orbis Books, 2013), 452–62.

11. For more on the general subject, see *Merton and Sufism: A Complete Compendium*, ed. Rob Baker and Gray Henry (Louisville, KY: Fons Vitae Press, 1999).

> . . . is to uncover this "yes" so that my life is totally
> and completely an assent to God. . . . It is while
> constantly saying "yes" that the contemplative life
> is an inner "yes" itself.
>
> Merton says that God gives us the potential for
> saying this yes. . . . All we need to do is turn toward
> it and let it become a flame.[12]

The same complex of ideas occurs almost verbatim
in a talk Merton gave to sisters in Alaska before he left
for Asia.[13] There he said, "Sufism looks at man as a
heart and a spirit and as a secret, and the secret is the
deepest part. . . . My secret is God's innermost knowledge of me, which He alone possesses. It is God's secret
knowledge of myself in Him."[14] According to Merton,
the "secret" is the word "yes" or the act of "yes." "My
destiny in life . . . is to uncover this 'yes' so that my

---

12. The talk is reprinted in *Hidden in the Same Mystery: Thomas
Merton and Loretto*, ed. Bonnie Thurston (Louisville, KY: Fons Vitae
Press, 2010), 63–80. Quotation is on p. 72. The conferences Merton
presented to religious women in the autumn of 1968 were subsequently sequentially printed in vol. 42 (1970–1971) of *Sisters Today*.

13. For more on Merton in Alaska, see Kathleen Witkowska Tarr,
*We Are All Poets Here: Thomas Merton's 1968 Journey to Alaska—A
Shared Story about Spiritual Seeking* (Anchorage, AK: VP&D House,
2017), and Bonnie Thurston, "Islam in Alaska: Sufi Material in
Thomas Merton in Alaska," *The Merton Seasonal* 29, no. 4 (Winter
2004): 3–8.

14. Robert E. Daggy, ed., *Thomas Merton in Alaska* (New York:
New Directions, 1989), 153.

life is totally and completely a 'yes' to God, a complete assent to God. . . . Deep in our hearts is the most profound meaning of our personality, which is that we say 'yes' to God, and the spark is always there. All we need to do is to turn towards it and let it become a flame."[15] Our deepest identity is a "given," the gift of "yes" that God offers to each person and longs to have returned. Our most authentic self, like that of our Lady, returns to its Creator this "yes." The whole monastic project, *conversio morum*, is to encourage this turning to God, this personal "yes." The monastic life encourages the "yes." The individual monk must come volitionally to it.

In a section of *Conjectures of a Guilty Bystander* aptly titled "The Fork in the Road," Merton suggests that to "make that turn" is to model Christ's own gift of "yes" to God. He writes, "One must live as a Christian, act as a Christian, with a life and an activity which spring from the unconditional 'yes' of Christ to the Father's will, incarnated in our own unconditional 'yes' to the reality, truth, and love which are made fully accessible to us in the Person and the Cross of Christ."[16] He continues, "My life and action seek their meaning in a world which has been reconciled with its own truth and its origin by Christ's love for it and for His Father."[17]

15. Daggy, ed., *Thomas Merton in Alaska*, 154.

16. Thomas Merton, *Conjectures of a Guilty Bystander* (Garden City, NY: Doubleday/Image, 1966/1968), 267–68.

17. Merton, *Conjectures*, 268.

Some Practical Applications

Merton taught that within each one of us is a "primordial *yes* that is not our own" (italics in original).[18] But we must freely choose it. Put crudely, it is our choosing that activates the "yes" that is (now repeating and quoting Merton) "a complete, trusting, and abandoned consent to the 'yes' of God in Christ." Our own "unconditional 'yes'" is "made fully accessible to us in the Person and in the Cross of Christ."[19] God longs for it, but the choice is ours.

We have had reason to quote Dag Hammarskjold earlier in this study. His journal entry for Whitsunday (Pentecost) 1961 precisely exemplifies Merton's point. Hammarskjold writes, "I don't know Who—or what—put the question. I don't know when it was put. I don't even remember answering. But at some moment I did answer *Yes* to Someone—or Something—and from that hour I was certain that existence is meaningful and that, therefore, my life, in self-surrender, had a goal."[20]

This crucial "yes" is at the heart of prayer. If we accept what Sr. Mary Luke Tobin reported in the talk previously mentioned, this is the *essence* of prayer. In *Contemplation in a World of Action* Merton pens this

18. Merton, *Conjectures*, 266.
19. Merton, *Conjectures*, 267–68.
20. Dag Hammarskjold, *Markings* (New York: Alfred A. Knopf, 1964), 205.

striking definition of prayer: "Prayer is *freedom and affirmation* growing out of nothingness into love" (italics mine). Prayer is "the elevation of our limited freedom into the infinite freedom of the divine spirit, and of the divine love."[21] Divine Love always launches us into a "world of action." The choice to say "yes," to give our total creative consent, is not for our own sake alone. It's not just a choice with private consequences (although they are manifold). When we say our "yes," give our *fiat*, we become implicated in, indeed responsible for, the ongoing resurrection that began with Mary's "yes" and with Jesus whose resurrection was God's "Big YES."

"Creative consent" is linked with commitment to God's intended justice, mercy, and peace for the whole creation, all those things for which Mary praised God in her *Magnificat*: God's looking with favor on a lowly servant and demonstration of mercy in scattering the proud, bringing down the powerful, lifting up the lowly, filling the hungry, and sending the rich away empty (see Luke 1:47-55). Creative consent, our "yes," enacts the Gospel. Merton explained, "The Gospel is the news that, if I will, I can respond now in perfect freedom to the redemptive love of God . . . in Christ, that I can *now* rise above the forces of necessity and evil in order to say 'yes' to the mysterious action of Spirit that is transforming the world even in the midst of the

21. Merton, *Contemplation in a World of Action*, 345.

violence and confusion and destruction that seem to proclaim His absence and his 'death.' "[22]

The point of all this is that, like that astonishing woman in St. Oran's Chapel, no matter how young or old or able or impaired we are, whether we are monastics or not, we can rise up saying "yes, Yes, YES." To reprise a theme introduced in chapter 4, that very affirmation implicates us in action for and movement toward the reign of God that the birth of Jesus inaugurated.

Conclusion

In a letter of August 5, 1968, to Mother Myriam Dardenne at Redwoods monastery, after what now seems an eerie aside ("I may never get back from Asia"), Merton pens a comment that recapitulates much of what I hope was suggested in this book: "[A]ll the monastic traditions have this in common: total liberation and availability to 'let go' and open up to the unspoken silence in which all is said: *qui erat et qui est et qui venturus est* [who was and who is and who shall come]" (italics and translation in original).[23] Both monastic spirituality and Christian spirituality at its core are about liberation, the freedom both to open up to what is as

22. Merton, *Conjectures*, 128.
23. Thomas Merton, *The School of Charity: Letters on Religious Renewal and Spiritual Direction*, ed. Patrick Hart (New York: Harvest/HBJ Book, 1990), 393.

yet unknown (represented in the quotation by silence) and to assist others to become more free.

Finally, it seems appropriate to draw this brief study of Merton's monastic spirituality, a spirituality that has implications and applications for all Christians, to a close with two quotations from monastic sources that were especially important to Merton. The first is from the fourth-century Desert Father, Abbot Joseph, whom Merton included in *Wisdom of the Desert*. And the second is the closing lines of the Prologue of the Rule of St. Benedict, who should, of course, naturally be given the last word.

> Abbot Lot came to Abbot Joseph and said: Father, according as I am able, I keep my little rule, and my little fast, my prayer, meditation and contemplative silence; and according as I am able I strive to cleanse my thoughts: now what more should I do? The elder rose up in reply and stretched out his hands to heaven, and his fingers became like ten lamps of fire. He said: Why not be totally changed into fire?[24]

Why not, indeed? If we blow ever so slightly on the ember of our life's "yes," all of us, monastic or not, may

24. Thomas Merton, *The Wisdom of the Desert: Sayings from the Desert Fathers of the Fourth Century* (New York: New Directions, 1960), 50.

become fire, in the words of the Easter Vigil's *Exsultet*: "The light of Christ." Any number of spiritual writers, especially those in the Orthodox Christian tradition, have noted the "light" that emanates from those of increasing holiness. Dom Michael Casey says this genuine holiness is "somaticized" and becomes evident in the physical appearance. Casey quotes William of Saint-Thierry, "The interior light shines forth in their outer countenance," and notes that "[t]he transformation of the saints is not merely for their own benefit—they are intended to be sources of light and encouragement for us."[25] When we catch fire, we become light for others.

And so, finally, the words of St. Benedict: "As we progress in this way of life and in faith, we shall run on the path of God's commandments, our hearts overflowing with the inexpressible delight of love. . . . [W]e shall through patience share in the sufferings of Christ that we may deserve also to share in his kingdom."[26]

25. Michael Casey, *Strangers to the City* (Brewster, MA: Paraclete Press, 2013/2018), 187.

26. *The Rule of St. Benedict*, 165, 167.

Thomas Merton and Monasticism: A Select Descriptive Bibliography

Most of Merton's published writings are monastic since their author was a monk who lived in a monastery. An extensive bibliography of Merton's work has been masterfully produced by Patricia A. Burton, *More Than Silence: A Bibliography of Thomas Merton* (ATLA Bibliography Series 55 [Lanham, MD: The Scarecrow Press, 2008]). The Thomas Merton Center at Bellarmine University in Louisville, Kentucky, is the primary repository of Merton's papers and of secondary material. Its website, www.Merton.org, is an online source for Merton studies and the link to *The Merton Seasonal* of the International Thomas Merton Society (which updates Merton bibliography quarterly), *The Merton Annual* (USA), and *The Merton Journal* (Great Britain and Ireland, link, www.thomasmertonsociety .org.uk). Recordings of Merton's talks at Gethsemani, as well as some other talks, are archived at the Thomas Merton Center. Many are available from www.Now YouKnowMedia.com. The indispensible one-volume source for Merton information is William H. Shannon, Christine M. Bochen, Patrick F. O'Connell, eds., *The Thomas Merton Encyclopedia* (Maryknoll, NY: Orbis Books, 2002).

Biographies of Merton

Many exist. Several are interpretive, "Merton and" biographies reflecting the interests of the biographers. Michael Mott's *The Seven Mountains of Thomas Merton* (Boston: Houghton Mifflin, 1984) was undertaken with the cooperation of the Merton Legacy Trust. It is massive (690 pages), detailed, and perhaps provides more than a general reader requires. My personal preferences are the biographies written by dean of Merton studies, William H. Shannon (of blessed memory). His *Silent Lamp: The Thomas Merton Story* (New York: Crossroad, 1992) places events in Merton's life in the context of historical events of his time. Shannon wrote *'Something of a Rebel': Thomas Merton, His Life and Works; An Introduction* (Cincinnati, OH: St. Anthony Messenger Press, 1997) for a popular audience. (The 2005 edition is titled *Thomas Merton: An Introduction*.) Those interested in a biography by one who knew Merton personally and that includes many photographs will enjoy Jim Forest's *Living with Wisdom: A Life of Thomas Merton*, revised edition (Maryknoll, NY: Orbis Books, 2008). Esther de Waal's *A Seven Day Journey with Thomas Merton* (Cincinnati, OH: Servant Books/

St. Anthony Messenger Press, 1992) introduces Merton by means of a personal retreat and includes many of his photographs. The overview of his life and introduction to his work in *Thomas Merton: Essential Writings* (Maryknoll, NY: Orbis Books, 2000) by the editor Christine M. Bochen are excellent and elegant. In my view, it is the best general introduction to Merton.

Merton Books on Monastic Life Published in His Lifetime

Basic Principles of Monastic Spirituality. Trappist, KY: Abbey of Gethsemani, 1957, and Springfield, IL: Templegate Publishers, 1996.

Disputed Questions. New York: Farrar, Straus & Cudahy, 1960. Part 3.

The Last of the Fathers: Saint Bernard of Clairvaux and the Encyclical Letter, Doctor Mellifluus. New York: Harcourt, Brace, 1954.

The Sign of Jonas. New York: Harcourt, Brace, 1953. He selected from journals of 1946–1952.

The Silent Life. New York: Farrar, Straus & Cudahy, 1957.

The Waters of Siloe. New York: Harcourt, Brace, 1949.

The Wisdom of the Desert: Sayings from the Desert Fathers of the Fourth Century. New York: New Directions, 1960.

Additionally, Merton wrote biographies of Cistercian women, *Exile Ends in Glory* (Mother M. Berchmans) (Milwaukee, WI: The Bruce Publishing Company, 1948) and *What Are These Wounds?* (St. Lutgarde of Aywieres) (Milwaukee, WI: The Bruce Publishing Company, 1950). In February 1967 he rated them (respectively) as "very poor" and "awful"; however, they are part of his monastic work and interesting as "period pieces." Merton also wrote a number of shorter works on monasticism that were published by the Abbey of Gethsemani and that are not included here.

Merton's journals and letters were written by a monk. The seven volumes of Merton's journals published by HarperSanFrancisco between 1995 and 1998 are arguably monastic documents. The same is true for collections of Merton's letters, especially *Thomas Merton, The School of Charity: Letters on Religious Renewal and Spiritual Direction*, ed. Br. Patrick Hart (New York: Harvest/HBJ Book, 1990) and *Survival or Prophecy? The Letters of Thomas Merton & Jean Leclercq*, ed. Patrick Hart (New York: Farrar, Straus & Giroux, 2002). One can explore Merton's journals, essays, and letters in the following well-edited, genre collections:

The Intimate Merton: His Life from His Journals. Edited by Patrick Hart and Jonathan Montaldo. San Francisco: Harper/SanFrancisco, 1999.

Thomas Merton: A Life in Letters. Edited by William H. Shannon and Christine M. Bochen. New York: Harper One, 2008.

Thomas Merton: Selected Essays. Edited by Patrick F. O'Connell. Maryknoll, NY: Orbis Books, 2013.

Merton's Monastic Materials
Edited after His Death

The Monastic Wisdom Series, an imprint of Cistercian Publications is issuing versions of Merton's talks to his novices at Gethsemani. They are edited by Patrick F. O'Connell, whose commentary on the material is invaluable for students of monasticism. The series is ongoing.

Thomas Merton. *Cassian and the Fathers.* Edited by Patrick F. O'Connell. Monastic Wisdom 1. Kalamazoo, MI: Cistercian Publications, 2005.

———. *Charter, Customs, and Constitutions of the Cistercians: Initiation into the Monastic Tradition 7.* Edited by Patrick F. O'Connell. Monastic Wisdom 41. Collegeville, MN: Cistercian Publications, 2015.

———. *Cistercian Fathers and Forefathers: Essays and Conference.* Edited by Patrick F. O'Connell. Hyde Park, NY: New City Press, 2018.

———. *The Cistercian Fathers and Their Monastic Theology: Initiation into the Monastic Tradition 8.* Edited by Patrick F. O'Connell. Monastic Wisdom 42. Collegeville, MN: Cistercian Publications, 2016.

———. *The Climate of Monastic Prayer.* Collegeville, MN: Liturgical Press, 2018. Originally published *The Climate of Monastic Prayer.* Cistercian Studies 1. Washington, DC: Cistercian Publications, 1969.

———. *Contemplation in a World of Action.* Garden City, NY: Doubleday Image, 1973.

———. *Day of a Stranger*. Salt Lake City: Gibbs M. Smith, Inc., 1981.

———. *In the Valley of Wormwood: Cistercian and Blessed and Saints of the Golden Age*. Edited by Patrick Hart. Cistercian Studies 233. Collegeville, MN: Cistercian Publications, 2013.

———. *The Life of the Vows: Initiation into the Monastic Tradition 6*. Edited by Patrick F. O'Connell. Monastic Wisdom 30. Collegeville, MN: Cistercian Publications, 2012.

———. *Medieval Cistercian History: Initiation into the Monastic Tradition 9*. Edited by Patrick F. O'Connell. Monastic Wisdom 43. Collegeville, MN: Cistercian Publications, 2019.

———. *The Monastic Journey*. Edited by Patrick Hart. Kalamazoo, MI: Cistercian Publications, 1977.

———. *Monastic Observances: Initiation into the Monastic Tradition 5*. Edited by Patrick F. O'Connell. Monastic Wisdom 25. Collegeville, MN: Cistercian Publications, 2010.

———. *Pre-Benedictine Monasticism: Initiation into the Monastic Tradition 2*. Edited by Patrick F. O'Connell. Monastic Wisdom 9. Kalamazoo, MI: Cistercian Publications, 2006.

———. *The Rule of Saint Benedict: Initiation into the Monastic Tradition 4*. Edited by Patrick F. O'Connell. Monastic Wisdom 19. Collegeville, MN: Cistercian Publications, 2009.

————. *The Springs of Contemplation: A Retreat at the Abbey of Gethsemani.* Edited by Jane Marie Richardson. New York: Farrar, Straus & Giroux, 1992.

Thomas Merton on Saint Bernard. Edited by Patrick Hart. Cistercian Studies 9. Kalamazoo, MI: Cistercian Publications, 1980.

Thomas Merton: The School of Charity (Letters on Religious Renewal and Spiritual Direction). Edited by Patrick Hart. New York: Harvest/HBJ Book, 1990.

Secondary Book-Length Studies of Merton the Monk

Hundreds of dissertations, books, and articles on Merton, many treating aspects of Merton the monk or Merton the monastic teacher exist. To locate them consult *About Merton: Secondary Sources 1945–2000*, edited by Marquita E. Breit, Patricia A. Burton, and Paul M. Pearson (Louisville, KY: The Thomas Merton Foundation, 2002) and the website www.Merton.org, maintained by the Thomas Merton Center. Books listed below are accessible studies focused on Merton the monk, and three are by his Cistercian confreres.

Bamberger, John Eudes. *Thomas Merton: Prophet of Renewal.* Monastic Wisdom 4. Collegeville, MN: Cistercian Publications, 2005.

Cunningham, Lawrence S. *Thomas Merton and the Monastic Vision.* Grand Rapids, MI: Eerdmans, 1999.

Grayston, Donald, *Thomas Merton and the Noonday Demon: The Camaldoli Correspondence*. Eugene, OR: Cascade Books, 2015.

Hart, Patrick. *Thomas Merton, Monk: A Monastic Tribute*. New York: Sheed & Ward, 1974. Enlarged edition, Cistercian Studies 52. Kalamazoo, MI: Cistercian Publications, 1983.

Lipsey, Roger. *Make Peace Before the Sun Goes Down: The Long Encounter of Thomas Merton and His Abbot, James Fox*. Boston: Shambhala, 2015.

Pennington, M. Basil. *Thomas Merton: Brother Monk*. San Francisco: Harper & Row, 1987.

In addition to Morgan Atkinson's DVD, *Gethsemani*, the following books provide visual orientation to Merton's monastery, its geography, and considerable influence on his monastic development.

Aprile, Dianne. *The Abbey of Gethsemani: Place of Peace and Paradox*. Louisville, KY: Trout Lily Press, 1998.

Casey, Michael, and Clyde F. Crews. *Monks Road: Gethsemani into the Twenty-First Century*. Trappist, KY: Abbey of Gethsemani, 2015.

Hinkle, Harry L., and Monica Weis. *Thomas Merton's Gethsemani: Landscapes of Paradise*. Lexington, KY: University of Kentucky Press, 2005.

Acknowledgments
and Thanksgivings

Many people and experiences stand behind a book. My work on Merton builds on and is greatly indebted to that of Fr. William F. Shannon of gracious memory: gracious in sharing his knowledge and encouraging Merton studies at every level. I never complete a Merton project without help from Paul M. Pearson and/or Mark Meade of The Thomas Merton Center at Bellarmine University, Louisville, Kentucky. I do not take for granted their prompt, accurate responses and their seemingly infinite patience. Merton scholars owe them and bibliographer Patricia Burton a great deal. Patrick F. O'Connell and Paul M. Pearson provided invaluable suggestions for and corrections to this book's select bibliography. The erudition and friendship of Christine M. Bochen and Sr. Monica Weis, SSJ, have made me a better scholar and a happier person.

I am particularly grateful to the Benedictine Sisters of Mount Saint Benedict in Erie, Pennsylvania, who endured my talks on Merton and monastic life during their community retreat June 5–10, 2017, and to the Benedictine sisters at Emmanuel Monastery in Baltimore, Maryland, who invited me to reprise the talks for their retreat June 24–30, 2018. Their warm hospitality and positive responses encouraged me to think the material might be valuable to wider audiences.

To know monasticism one must be instructed by monastics. My life and prayer have been deeply influenced by the Cistercians to whom this book is gratefully dedicated and by the sisters of the Society of the Sacred Cross, Tymawr, Wales; the Trappistines (OCSO) of Our Lady of the Angels Monastery, Crozet, Virginia; and the Sisters of the Love of God, Oxford, England.

Although permissions were not strictly required, I thank the editors of *The Merton Annual*, *The Merton Seasonal* of the International Thomas Merton Society, and *The Merton Journal* of The Thomas Merton Society of Great Britain and Ireland who published earlier drafts of chapters 7, 8, and 10, respectively. (Full details are in the notes of those chapters.) Permission to use the quotation on page 130 by Brian Purfield that appeared on Day 3 of the online offering "31 Days of St Ignatius" (see www.pathwaystogod.org and https://www.pathwaystogod.org/31-days-st-ignatius-2019) has kindly been given by the author. Liturgical Press gave permission to use herein my poem on pages 142–43 from *Belonging to Borders*, which they published in 2011.

New Directions generously granted permission to use the following Merton poems in the text: (1) "The Reader" by Thomas Merton, from THE COLLECTED POEMS OF THOMAS MERTON, copyright ©1949 by Our Lady of Gethsemani Monastery. (2) "In Silence" by Thomas Merton, from THE COLLECTED POEMS OF THOMAS MERTON, copyright ©1957 by The Abbey of Gethsemani. (3) "Song: If You Seek . . . " by Thomas Merton, from THE COLLECTED POEMS OF THOMAS MERTON, copyright ©1963 by The Abbey of Gesthemani, Inc. Reprinted by permission of New Directions Publishing Corp. Their inclusion gives you, gentle reader, a much richer insight into Merton's thought.

New Directions also granted permission for the following: "Some Sayings of the Desert Fathers" and "The Wisdom of the Desert" by Thomas Merton, from THE WISDOM OF THE DESERT, copyright ©1960 by The Abbey of Gethsemani, Inc. Excerpts by Thomas Merton, from THOMAS MERTON IN ALASKA, copyright ©1988, 1989 by The Trustees of the Merton Legacy Trust. Reprinted by permission of New Directions Publishing Corp.

I am grateful for a long relationship with Liturgical Press and especially to editor Hans Christoffersen for taking a chance on this book, for enduring endless queries, and for always being a considerate and supportive editor even when he says no to a submission. It is no small gift to be able to reject a manuscript and remain friends with its author. Thanks to Colleen Stiller, who so very capably directed the final preparation of this manuscript, and to Tara Durheim, who is making it known.

Profoundest thanks to Patrick F. O'Connell, longtime friend and erudite and exacting Merton scholar. He may know more about Merton and his publication history than anyone. He is certainly in the top three! Pat kindly and generously read the final draft of this manuscript and corrected errors minute and major, thereby saving me from a red and egg-ridden face and giving you a much better book than otherwise you would have had. Any remaining errors, mistakes, or infelicities are "my own most grievous fault."

I undertook serious study of Thomas Merton as a doctoral candidate at the University of Virginia in 1976 and wrote my dissertation on Merton under the direction of Professor Raymond Nelson. Many of the joys and extraordinary opportunities of my life trace their origins directly to study of Thomas Merton. I have read and thought about Merton for a long time. Familiarity can breed forgetfulness. I may unintentionally have neglected to cite a source and will gratefully correct that error in any future editions of the book. I am grateful to you for reading it and hope you find encouragement and sustenance from Merton's life and monastic wisdom.